THE RIGHT HONOURABLE
Caroline Countess of Seafield

Born 30th June 1830.
Died 6th October 1911

*Mostly Reprinted from
Banffshire Journals of October 10 and 17, 1911*

The Portrait of the Countess of Seafield is reproduced from the "Rulers of Strathspey," by Lord Cassillis.

C7
T88
S4R5

CONTENTS.

	Page
SKETCH OF LIFE	3
FUNERAL	43
PULPIT REFERENCES	75
Abernethy Parish Church	91
Abernethy United Free Church	92
Advie Parish Church	90
Banff Parish Church	83
Boyndie Parish Church	84
Cromdale Parish Church	90
Cromdale United Free Church	91
Cullen Parish Church	75
Cullen United Free Church	77
Deskford Parish Church	78
Deskford United Free Church	79
Findochty United Free Church	85
Fordyce Parish Church	122
Fordyce United Free Church	81
Grantown Seafield Memorial Church	86
Grantown United Free Church	89
Grantown Baptist Church	89
Keith Parish Church	85
Keith North United Free Church	86
Kincardine Parish Church	92
Portsoy Parish Church	82
Portsoy East United Free Church	81
Portsoy St John's Church	82
Seafield Parish Church	80
TRIBUTES BY PUBLIC BODIES	93
Aberdeen Synod	95
Aberdeen-Angus Cattle Society	107
Abernethy Parish Council	118
Banffshire County Council	93
Banffshire Conservative Association	114
Banff Town Council	96

	Page
Banff Burgh School Board	103
Birnie Parish Council	111
Birnie School Board	118
Boyndie School Board	103
Boyndie Parish Council	117
Central Banffshire Farmer Club	108
Cromdale Parish Council	106
Cullen Town Council	98
Cullen School Board	105
Cullen Parish Council	116
Cullen Curling Club	109
Deskford Parish Council	106
Duthil and Rothiemurchus Parish Council	121
Elginshire County Council	94
Fordyce School Board	104
Forres Town Council	100
Forres and Northern Fat Cattle Club	109
Grantown Town Council	101
Grantown Amenities Committee	112
Keith Town Council	99
Keith Parish Council	117
Keith Curling Club	112
Northern Seeds and Roots Association	115
Portsoy Town Council	100
Presbytery of Fordyce	121
Rothes Town Council	101
Rothes School Board	115
Rothes Bowling Club	113
Rothes Curling Club	117
Rothes Parish Council	120
Seafield Memorial Church, Inverallan	110
Urquhart and Glenmoriston School Board	119
Urquhart and Glenmoriston Parish Council	119

THE LATE LADY SEAFIELD.

With deep regret we announce to-day the death of the venerable and venerated lady who for so many years has administered with rare ability and discrimination the great and widely-extended affairs of the House of Seafield, and who has occupied with distinction and with the sympathy and affection of all one of the greatest positions in the North of Scotland. The sad event had not been altogether unlooked for, although it must come to many as if with a sense of personal bereavement, so familiar was her ladyship's name over a wide territory in the northern counties, and such was the place of respectful affection and esteem in which her high qualities of heart and mind were held. In the spring of last year Lady Seafield suffered a very serious illness, felt all the more, as was natural, in view of the years to which she had attained On that occasion, much to the gratification of all, she made a wonderful recovery, and in course her ladyship regained something of her old elasticity Of late, however, weakness had returned in an accentuated form. She had been able to take short walks near Cullen House, and up to Wednesday, although then quite confined to her room, was able to attend to business, signing papers on that day Her ladyship's weakness was, however, very great, and on Friday morning, shortly after six o'clock, the worst fears were realised, when the much-loved Countess, a noble lady whose name will linger long in many associations of the north country which had been for so long her home, passed to her rest. Retired though she had been for long from public activities of most kinds, her removal causes a void that will be for long keenly felt.

Numerous messages of condolence and sympathy were received at Cullen House on Friday. One of the earliest was from His Majesty King George, who had known Lady Seafield for many years, and of whose death he heard with deep regret The King met her ladyship frequently at Castle Grant, and had also visited the Countess at Cullen House. To-morrow the remains are to be removed from Cullen House to Castle Grant They will be there over night in the stately Highland home of the family, and on Thursday they will be deposited in the family mausoleum at the church of Duthil on that beautiful Speyside which her ladyship loved so well, but which, much to her regret, she had not been able to visit for some years.

LADY SEAFIELD'S FAMILY.

The Right Hon. Caroline Stuart, Countess of Seafield, was born 30th June 1830, and was twin with a brother Henry, who died April 13, 1842 She was the youngest of eleven children born to Robert Walter, 11th Lord Blantyre and his wife, Fanny Mary, second daughter of the Hon. John Rodney, son of the celebrated Admiral Lord Rodney. The future Countess of Seafield belonged to a very ancient family—the Stuarts of Minto, for many years hereditary provosts of Glasgow, and subsequently Lords Blantyre. That family was founded by Thomas Stuart, a cadet of the Stuarts of Garlies, Earls of Galloway. In 1476 he owned lands in Lanarkshire and elsewhere. He died in 1500 and was buried before the altar of Our Lady in the cathedral of Aberdeen He was succeeded by his son John, who was knighted in 1508. The eldest surviving son of the third subsequent generation was Walter Stuart, known for long under the designation of the Prior of Blantyre. He was brought up along with James VI., under George Buchanan, and had the Priory of Blantyre bestowed on him by that monarch. On the death of Buchanan he got the office of Privy Seal, and it is a curious coincidence, in view of a later act of State by an Earl of Seafield, that this ancestor of the Countess of Seafield should have in December 1604 signed the abortive treaty of that Union which was not destined to be carried into effect for another century. In 1606 he was raised to the Peerage under the title of Lord Blantyre and died in 1617. His eldest son, Sir James Stuart, fought a duel at Islington with the eldest son of Lord Wharton on 8th November 1609. Both combatants were killed on the spot, and were, by the King's command, interred in one grave in the churchyard there. The first Lord Blantyre was succeeded therefore by his second son, William, who was created a Knight of the Bath in 1610 He was succeeded in turn by his two sons, Walter and Alexander, the former dying without issue The latter was one of the "Engagers" who offered in 1647 to put the arms of Scotland at the disposal of Charles I. His son Alexander, fifth Lord Blantyre, gave a practical proof of his adherence to the Hanoverian Government by raising a regiment of six hundred Foot, and got a commission as its colonel In 1702 he succeeded to the estate of his relative, the Duchess of Richmond and Lennox—the cheery and vivacious beauty of the court of Charles II., who has come down to us as "La Belle Stuart" That lady bequeathed the bulk of her property to her relative, the fifth Lord Blantyre, for the purchase of certain estates to be called "Lennox's love to Blantyre." He purchased accordingly the estate of Lethington in Haddingtonshire, and changed its name to Lennoxlove. Bothier, the engraver to the Royal Mint, executed a medal of her, and she served as model for the figure of Britannia on the copper coins The fifth Lord Blantyre was succeeded in turn by his eldest and second sons—Walter, who voted against the Union in Parliament but was afterwards chosen one of the sixteen Representative Scottish Peers at the general election in 1710, and Robert, seventh Lord Blantyre, who was a captain of a regiment of Foot, and was serving in Minorca when the succession opened to him He died in 1743, and was succeeded in turn by three sons—Walter, who resided much abroad, and was a scholar, and died at Paris in 1751; William, who was a colonel in the service of the States of Holland, and Alexander, tenth Lord Blantyre, who resided at Erskine, and took much interest in the management of his estates and in agriculture generally. His eldest son, Robert Walter, eleventh Lord Blantyre, was the father of the lady who has just passed away He was born in 1775 He served in Holland in 1799, in Egypt in 1801, in the expedition to Pomerania and Zealand in 1807, and in the Peninsular War in 1809, rising to the rank of lieutenant-general In 1806 he was elected one of the sixteen Scottish Representative Peers, and was for some time Lord-Lieutenant of Renfrewshire He was accidentally killed by a shot fired during the Revolution in Brussels while looking out of the window of his hotel there, on 22nd September 1830, three months after the birth of his daughter Caroline. The eldest son of the family, Charles Walter, twelfth Lord Blantyre, died in 1900, when the Barony became extinct, having been predeceased by his only son Walter, who died, unmarried, in 1895

EARL OF SEAFIELD'S FAMILY

The lady who has just passed away at Cullen House came therefore of distinguished lineage, members of successive generations having served the State for long in active work in the field or in Parliament. Her marriage to John Charles, a future Earl of Seafield, was celebrated on 12th August 1850. The bride was then twenty years of age, and for the long period of one and sixty years she was destined in days that saw much happiness and much sorrow to be identified in a most intimate and responsible way with vast interests throughout the North of Scotland. The family into which she then entered was of ancient line, and members of it had distinguished themselves in many spheres of public action. The bridegroom was then Viscount Reidhaven, eldest son of the Earl of Seafield. He was the representative of two great families boasting high antiquity—the Grants and the Findlater branch of the Ogilvies. As head of the Grants he could trace his lineage in an unbroken series of male descent for six hundred years. He was the twenty-second in direct male descent from Sir Duncan de Grant, who held lands in Banffshire, and was grandson of Gregory de Grant, who was Sheriff of Inverness in the early part of the thirteenth century. The Findlater branch of the Ogilvies are sprung from Sir Walter Ogilvie of Auchleven, second son of a knight of the same name, who in 1425 was Lord High Treasurer of Scotland. By marrying in 1437 the daughter and heiress of Sir John Sinclair of Deskford and Findlater, Sir Walter Ogilvie acquired these lands, and the sixth in descent from him, also a Sir Walter, was elevated to the Peerage under the title of Baron Ogilvie of Deskford. Lord Ogilvie's son was in 1638 created Earl of Findlater. The fourth Earl of Findlater was a lawyer of great eminence and filled the offices of Secretary of State for Scotland, Lord Chief Baron of the Exchequer, and Chancellor of Scotland. The proposals for the Union of Scotland and England were brought to a successful conclusion mainly owing to his indefatigable industry, ability and address. Previous to that event he was created Earl of Seafield and Viscount Reidhaven. The second Earl of Seafield made handsome provision for the Duke of Cumberland's troops when on their way to Culloden. The third Earl travelled much in his youth. Horace Walpole, who met him at Rome in 1740, writing to his friend Conway, says—"You saw Lord Deskford at Geneva. Don't you like him? He is a mighty sensible man There are few young men have so good an understanding" On succeeding to the estates in 1764, the Earl fixed his residence at Cullen House and took a lead in everything of importance in the country. He may be said to have introduced the rotation of cropping and was the first to sow turnips in the field as a regular crop He laid off several model farms, he squared the fields and built excellent fences. He died in 1770, leaving a son, by whom he was succeeded, and who died without issue on 5th October 1811, when the Findlater Earldom and the Viscountcy of Seafield expired The succession to the Earldom of Seafield then opened up to the descendants of Lady Margaret, the elder daughter of James, fifth Earl of Findlater and second Earl of Seafield. This lady married Sir Ludovic Grant of Grant, by whom, besides daughters, she had one son, Sir James Grant He left two sons, the elder of whom, Sir Lewis Alexander Grant, on the death of the last Earl of Findlater and fourth Earl of Seafield, in October 1811, succeeded as fifth Earl of Seafield His lordship died unmarried, and was succeeded by his younger brother, Francis William, who was the father of the peer who on August 12, 1850, married the Hon. Caroline Stuart. He was born at Cullen House on 4th September 1815 For eleven years he served in the Royal Navy, and on the death of his elder brother, the Master of Grant, on 11th March 1840, he retired from the service, and his father having succeeded in the same year to the Earldom, he assumed the title of Viscount Reidhaven.

LADY SEAFIELD'S WELCOME NORTH.

The marriage of the heir to the vast estates of the Seafield family was the occasion of great rejoicings in the North, where the bride was joyfully welcomed and where for six decades her name has in wide districts been a household word for tender womanly sympathy and for devotion to the duties of her exalted position. Some of the doings of the day may be fitly recalled, for what was done then introduced to northern life a lady who was for long to exercise a most powerful and wholly beneficent influence in all its manifold affairs, and who has over her great estates left an impression for good that many years will not efface. At Cullen there was a great display of flags. Many of the inhabitants, wearing marriage favours, and, preceded by school children, met at Duncan's Hall and marched to Cullen House, where cheers were given for the noble Viscount and Viscountess. The procession went on to the old castle hill and took their station around the old Cross of the burgh where more cheers were given. A dinner, attended by 150 people, took place in the afternoon in Watson's Hotel. The chair was occupied by Mr Alex. Wilson, Kilnhillock; the croupiers were Mr George Murray, Mossside; Mr John Taylor, sen., Brunton; and Dr Sharp, Cullen, and among those present were Rev. Mr Forbes, Boharm; Mr Wm. Anderson, Cullen; Dr Munro, Cullen; Dr Emslie, Banff; Mr John Wilson, Tochineal, and Rev. Mr Gardiner, Rathven. No fewer than seven and twenty toasts were honoured, beginning with Her Majesty the Queen and ending with a toast to the health of the parties who had met in the different districts for a similar purpose. Other townsmen of Cullen met at dinner in the Red Lion Hotel under the presidency of Provost Sinclair, and the croupiers here were Councillor Dunbar and Mr Wm Duffus. At night there were fireworks, and in Duncan's Hall a ball was held. At Banff the shipping had their flags hoisted. In the afternoon over one hundred gentlemen met at dinner in Gillander's Hotel. The chair was occupied by Mr Andrew Longmore, jun., Baldavie, who was supported by Mr F. G. Sangster, Rev. R. G. Bremner, Captain Grant, Glenbarry; Mr G. C. Smith, land surveyor; Rev. Mr Grant, Ordiquhill, Dr Gordon, R.N.; Mr E. Mortimer, and Mr Adam, banker. At Portsoy a dinner was held in Mr Minty's hall, while the ladies of the town held an open air tea party on the lawn adjoining the house of Durn. At the dinner Mr Peter Murray presided, and Mr Tait, North Mains, was croupier. Some of those present were Rev. Mr Murray, Mr Robert Wilson, Brangan; Rev. John Gaul, Mr John Morrison, Whyntie; Mr Stevenson, Smiddyboyne; Mr Donaldson, Auchip, and Mr Stevenson, Toux. At night there was a great bonfire on the Square, composed of a couple of boats, brush wood, and tar barrels. There was a bonfire on the hill of Baldavie. At Fordyce there was dinner in the New Inn, presided over by Mr Walter Gray, who was supported by Rev. Mr Innes, minister of the parish, and Rev. Mr Stephen. At night there was a bonfire on the hill of Fordyce. The Rathven tenantry marched to the Moor of Rannes, where there was a bonfire, and in Mr Simpson's loft there a dinner party was held. In Deskford, there was a bonfire at Fechy Hill, and at Moss-side a ball. The tenants on the estates of Crombie and Cranna, in Marnoch, met at dinner in Mr Robson's Inn at Aberchirder. At Keith a dinner party was presided over by Mr Wm Thurburn, and Mr W. Longmore was croupier. Among those present were Sheriff Currie, Rev. Mr Sellar, Aberlour; and Mr Roy, Avochie. There was a ball at night and on the marketplace there was a bonfire. At Bishopmill, Elgin, of which the Earl of Seafield was Superior, salutes were fired from a couple of cannon In Strathspey there were great rejoicings. Highland games were held in the Square of Grantown, and at dinner in the Court House the chair was occupied by Captain Grant, Congash At Elchies there was a bonfire and a ball. At Rothes the wedding day was observed as a holiday. At a dinner held there, Provost Grant of Elgin presided, Mr P Brown, Linkwood, was croupier, and among those present were Rev. Alex Asher, Inveraven; Mr John Fraser, Auchroisk; Mr Smith, Drumin, Mr Mantach, Dundurcas; and Mr Smith, distiller, Glenlivet. On the Inverness-shire estates the rejoicings were on an equally enthusiastic and extensive scale.

PUBLIC AND SOCIAL WORK.

That was the wholehearted way in which in August 1850 large areas throughout the North of Scotland welcomed the bride of the house of Stuart who had mingled her fortunes with the house of Grant. The only child of the marriage, Ian Charles, eighth Earl of Seafield, was born on 7th October 1851 On 30th July 1853, by the death of his father, Viscount Reidhaven succeeded to the title and estates, and as the wife of the Earl of Seafield, the lady whose death we deplore, naturally took a more prominent part in the activities of Society In 1853 Lord Seafield was elected a Representative Peer and had thereafter Parliamentary duties to discharge. In 1858 he was raised to the Peerage of the United Kingdom as Baron Strathspey of Strathspey, and in 1879 Her

Majesty the Queen conferred on him the Order of the Thistle—honours that were of course reflected on his Countess. Lord Seafield, who was an elder in the parish church of Inverallan, had, before the abolition of patronage, the livings of sixteen parishes in his gift and invariably dispensed his patronage conscientiously and with much discrimination and judgment. In recognition of his services to the Church, Lord Seafield was offered in 1858 the post of Lord High Commissioner to the General Assembly, but he declined the honour. He was also patron of numerous bursaries to schools and to the University, and it is well known that in the recipients of his bounty in these directions the Countess took a warm interest. In additions made to the family mansions of Cullen House and Balmacaan, and in general improvements effected throughout the estate, his lordship had always the affectionate advice and warm interest of the Countess, and no one more than she sympathised with his great efforts at afforestation in Strathspey. Upwards of sixty million of trees were planted under his lordship's direction, and the beneficent result is now to be seen in the beautifully wooded appearance of the country there, while to their presence may be due in part the mild climate with which that part of Speyside is endowed. The Earl and Countess spent usually a portion of every spring in London, but the rest of the year was passed between Cullen House, Castle Grant, and Balmacaan. For Balmacaan they had an especial affection. It was the place where they had spent the early years of their married life and every time they returned to it with renewed pleasure. At each of their residences they entertained select parties of guests, and in no sphere did the Countess of Seafield more winningly display her gracious gifts of manner than as the bright, polished and vivacious hostess of guests who were under the roof-tree of the Chieftain of the Clan Grant.

HEAVY BEREAVEMENTS.

Thus, nearly thirty-one years of happy married life passed in the faithful and conscientious discharge of social and public duties Then the Countess experienced a heavy blow Her father had died when she was only three months old; her mother had passed away in the year of her silver wedding. In the early days of 1881 her ladyship suffered the heavy bereavement of the loss of her husband. In February of that year a shooting party was entertained at Cullen House. On its last day, his lordship caught a cold which assumed the form of complicated bronchitis, and on the 18th his sufferings ended The deepest sympathy everywhere went out to the sorrowing lady who had, it was universally recognised, in every sense adorned the high position she had so nobly filled, and who had by her kind and gracious ways won the affection and esteem of all classes It was a mitigation of her grief to some extent that by her side was her deeply loved son, then just thirty years of age, and abounding in the highest promise that bright hopes and manly youth could afford. Then three short years were to pass and the afflicted mother was next to experience the bereavement that crowned her sorrows in the loss of her only child. When the sad event occurred, the tragic element it contained was recognised by all, and on the lonely widow and the bereft mother there was by all classes lavished a wealth of tender sympathy that deeply touched her ladyship and helped her materially in the repetition of the cruel blows to face the future and the duties of her high position with a resignation and courage and devotion that all know and that all to-day appreciate. Her son, Ian Charles, died in London on 31st March 1884, following on an operation for aneurism of the femoral artery of the right thigh He was a young nobleman of high moral purpose and distinguished gifts, and seemed to have before him a future that would reflect honour on his name and that would influence the well-being of the country Educated at Eton, his lordship entered the First Life Guards in his nineteenth year He retired from the service in 1877, and subsequently resided almost constantly on the estates. In 1872 his majority was celebrated throughout the property by a series of rejoicings on a scale that has had few parallels locally On the death of his father in 1884 he gave increased attention to the affairs of the estate, and sought by steps, of which the wisdom was proved by time, to meet those new conditions which British agriculture had in the 'Eighties to face His last public appearance indeed was at a gathering of agriculturists, when he opened two silos constructed on the farms of Woodside and Tochineal and addressed to the assembled landowners and farmers observations of a highly practical character, giving evidence of careful consideration of the subject and of a bent of mind towards this class of subjects which, with spared life, would have made him an authority and a leader on agricultural matters in the North In the fold of Highland cattle at Castle Grant and in the Aberdeen-Angus herd at Cullen House he took a lively interest, and in Strathspey planting under his lordship went on as vigorously as it had under his father He was presented with the freedom of the burgh of Cullen, the entry on the burgess ticket bearing that the honour was conferred "for the singular favour and regard the Provost and Magistrates bear to his lordship." Lord Seafield was an elder in the parish church of Inverallan and took a deep and abiding interest in religious affairs. For six years he was the honoured Convener of Inverness-shire. The bond of affection which united him and his mother was of a strength and tenderness almost passing belief, and the depth of love that subsisted between them only rendered the more intense the anguish of mind which the bereaved mother and widow was called to endure. Lord Seafield, it may now be recalled, was a warm friend of Prince Leopold, Duke of Albany, youngest son of Queen Victoria. The last Sunday of the year 1883 was spent by his lordship with His Royal Highness at Claremont, and it was a sad coincidence that the two young men should have been lying dead at the same time. Lord Seafield's funeral to the churchyard of Duthil was one of the largest ever seen in the North of Scotland It was attended by over two thousand people gathered from the extremities of four counties A special train that carried the mourners from Forres to Castle Grant consisted of forty-four carriages, drawn by three engines, and it brought only a section of the company that was present.

LATER EARLS OF SEAFIELD

By the death of this young nobleman, of high hopes and bright promise, the centre of many happy anticipations, the title of Baron Strathspey of Strathspey became extinct, and the Seafield titles passed to his uncle, the Hon James Grant of Mayne. He was born 27th December 1817 He served for some years in the Army and was captain of the 42nd Highlanders. He represented the counties of Moray and Nairn in the House of Commons from 1868 to 1874. He was created a Peer of the United Kingdom under the title of Baron Strathspey of Strathspey in June 1884 He married, first, Caroline Louisa, second daughter of Eyre Evans of Ashhill Towers, co.

Limerick, grand nephew of George, first Lord
Carbery, and by her had Francis William,
born 9th March 1847, who succeeded as tenth
Earl of Seafield on the death of his father on
June 5, 1888. He married 24th November 1874
Anne Trevor Corry, daughter of Major George
Evans. He held the title only from June until
his death in December 1888, when he was succeeded by his son, James, eleventh and present Earl of Seafield, then a boy of twelve
years of age. He was born April 18, 1876. He
spent all his early years in New Zealand, coming to this country for the first time when he
was twenty-three years of age, and shortly
thereafter he became an officer in the 3rd Bedfordshire Regiment. He married 22nd June
1898 Mary Elizabeth Nina, eldest daughter of
Joseph Henry Townend, M D, J.P., of Park
Terrace, Christ Church, New Zealand. Their
daughter, Lady Nina Caroline, was born in
1906.

GREAT MEMORIAL GIFTS

On the deeply lamented death of her son,
the great estates of the family came into the
possession of the Countess Dowager of Seafield, and in the distracting cares of the oversight of the vast interests of such a landed
property, her ladyship found some relief from
the anguish of the double bereavement she
had suffered. While that is true, it is the fact
also to say that to the last she bore on her
chastened countenance the marks of the sorrow she had had to meet. Yet it was all
borne bravely, in complete resignation to the
will of the Higher Power Who had so ordained matters, and while signs of the harrowed feelings wrought by the double stroke
of bereavement were visible, there was ever
on her countenance, too, a look of gentle and
tender winsomeness that inspired high feelings
of respectful affection in all who came into

contact with her attractive and beautiful character One of her ladyship's first duties when she again took up the threads of the work of life was to see set on foot plans that had been begun by her son and to take steps for the perpetuation of his memory and that of her husband in schemes of enduring utility Thus, fifteen months after his death, in May 1885 there was opened at Grantown-on-Spey the Ian Charles Hospital. The erection and endowment of such a hospital had been arranged by the Countess Dowager and her son. It had been little more than founded when the Earl died, and his sorrowing mother brought the undertaking to a completion All who know the capital of Strathspey know the place well. On each side of the entrance door of the hospital is a tablet On one is inscribed—"Erected and endowed by Ian Charles, eighth Earl of Seafield, and his mother, Caroline Stuart, Countess of Seafield, 1884," and on the other is inscribed—"Look upon mine afflictions and my pains and forgive all my sins. Psalms xxv and 18 God is love, 1st John iv and 16" The hospital was and is fitted with all necessary conveniences and comforts for the treatment and care of the sick, and has been of untold benefit to the Speyside district of the Seafield estates. Recognising, again, how over all the property there was felt with her ladyship deep and respectful sympathy in the sore trials that had befallen her, the Countess gave instructions for the preparation of a volume of Memoirs of her son, which included the biographies of his lordship that had been printed in northern newspapers, and a copy was presented to a large number of the tenantry, by whom it has always been held in great value as a memorial of one who had been cut down at the threshold of his life's work. To the parish churches on the estate also Lady Seafield gifted chaste and beautiful memorial tablets of her husband and son. Her ladyship also built at Grantown the beautiful Seafield Memorial Church—a new church for the parish of Inverallan, in which both her husband and her son had held the office of elder. On May 1, 1886, the Countess placed the memorial stone on the building and the formal dedication of the church for public worship then took place. The building was designed by Mr Alex Smith, Cullen House, private architect to her ladyship. It is Gothic in style and cruciform in plan. A panel at the top of a Gothic arch bears in large letters the inscription—" This church erected by Caroline Stuart, Countess of Seafield, for the service of God, in memory of her beloved husband and son, the seventh and eighth Earls of Seafield, 1884 " — the year in which the church was planned. A memorial plate bears the inscription—" This church was erected to the glory of God by Caroline Stuart, Countess of Seafield, in loving memory of her husband, John Charles, seventh Earl of Seafield, K T, 26th Chief of the Grants, who died 18th February 1881; and of their only child, Ian Charles, eighth Earl of Seafield, 27th Chief of the Grants, who died 31st March 1884. Presented by her to the Church of Scotland as the Parish Church of Inverallan. Consecrated to the public worship of God, 1st May 1886. Rev. John Thomson, D D, minister. Alexander Smith, architect." The church, as many readers are aware, is one of the prettiest in all the run of Spey. On the Seafield pew are some beautiful and very old carvings. The entire cost of this fine memorial to a husband and son was, we believe, about £7000. On the occasion of the dedication of the church, her ladyship was presented with a silver trowel from the trustees of the congregation, and with a Bible and Psalter and an address from the Kirk Session. Part of the address was in these terms—" Knowing no more acceptable or appropriate testimony, we ask your ladyship's acceptance of this Holy Book and Psalter for use in the church, with the prayer that the consolations and hopes which it reveals may continue to inspire, sustain, comfort and guide your ladyship all through your earthly career, and prepare you for an abundant entrance into the everlasting kingdom of our Lord and Saviour Jesus Christ " In June 1887 Lady Seafield was one of those present when there was opened a new hall in connection with the church, and in April 1903, through her generosity and kindness, the electric light was introduced both into the church and the Ian Charles Hospital

HEAD OF A GREAT ESTATE

Lady Seafield was called to the administration of a great landed estate at a critical juncture in the condition and prospects of British agriculture World-wide movements that had been in progress for some years made their influence fully felt early in the 'Eighties The great prairie lands in the western States of America were coming under cultivation; the era of vast cattle ranges was in its heyday, the chilling process as applied to beef had been perfected, and large steamers were equipped for the efficient and economical transport of food from the new hemisphere to the old The agriculture of Great Britain felt the pressure of the competition in the most acute fashion, for our ports were open to the produce of the world, and bargains in farm tenancies that had been made in the prosperous 'Seventies could only with difficulty be met in the troublous period that opened in the 'Eighties and was emphasised with increasing force as the decade advanced. The North of Scotland did not escape the agitation that ensued. It was the day of the Farmers' Alliance, the day when a far-reaching series of investigations and enquiries by such a body as the Morayshire Farmers' Club found that the new conditions demanded all over a reduction in rental of 33⅓ per cent, and when in many cases confidence was shaken in the whole future of the agricultural industry. It is the fact and only the sober fact to say that on the Seafield estate the situation was faced with true insight and calm courage. The agitation experienced in many parts of the country never on it found a home, but on the other hand the relations between the Countess and her numerous tenantry remained on as firm and cordial a basis as had ever existed on the estate. Having beside her sagacious, experienced and sympathetic counsellors, Lady Seafield considered the circumstances and wants of each case individually, and arrangements were made for the amelioration of conditions that even ten years before had not been anticipated by the most far-seeing. In some years of stress a general abatement of rent was generously given. In 1886, for instance, the Strathspey tenantry acknowledged with gratitude a reduction of 30 per cent of their rental, and in the same year in the Cullen House district, which includes such highly fertile areas as the Boyne and Findlater, there was spontaneously given a reduction of 10 per cent. That may be taken as typical of what occurred from time to time before the new basis was fully discovered for meeting the conditions that had to be faced. To take another instance of the generous and enlightened policy that has ever characterised the estate management. the turnip crop of 1891-2, it may be recalled, was in many parts of the country a more or less absolute failure. At the rent collection in June 1892 a handsome abatement was allowed in view of the fact, illustrating again her ladyship's desire to make her own interest and those of her tenantry one and the same. So lately as 1904 the tenantry in the Ord district met and sent a letter of thanks to the Countess for a further abatement on account of severe local conditions there. Instances such as these could be multiplied, but the effect of them all goes to provide explanation of the fact that the tenantry were proud of their generous and sympathetic proprietrix, and that she was in turn proud of having under her a body of skilful, enterprising and contented farmers, who regarded with feelings of gratitude the benefits her ladyship bestowed upon them for the more prosperous prosecution of their industry. Lady Seafield was a most able and prudent administrator of the great trust in her hands. Everything connected with the estate was maintained in a high degree of efficiency, and so far-seeing and eminently sagacious were her principles of management that this fact deserves and ought to be said that she has left the large property on a much sounder and more stable basis than it had previously been. We are not at liberty to mention details of facts that are known only to a few, but this broad statement has to be made that the benefits of her administration have been very great, and, in relation to the well-being of the estate, they have been of surpassing importance. Having on the estate many towns and villages, it was natural that appeals should be made from time to time to her ladyship by the communities for land for a variety of purposes. Church yards had to be extended or new cemeteries provided; bowling greens were wanted; land was wanted for the site of public buildings, and water rights had to be negotiated for the benefit of growing towns, but for whatever beneficent purpose it was wanted, no appeal was ever made in vain to her ladyship, who, mindful that she was administering for her lifetime a great trust, saw to it also that the terms on which the transaction took place were as favourable for the public weal as they could possibly be made. One of the most recent instances of her generosity in this respect was seen in January 1908, when the Countess presented the burgh of Keith with the market park of the town and adjoining plantation, extending in all to 12 acres, along with the right of exacting market dues. That is an asset of great and increasing value to Keith, and as the town increases, the provision of such a place for the purposes of a public park will ever the more be held in value. While speaking of this, reference may be made to the visit in June 1891 of the Countess of Seafield to Keith, when her ladyship was officially received by the Commissioners of the burgh. An address was then presented to her in the following terms:—

"We, the Commissioners of the police burgh of Keith, having learned that your ladyship purposes visiting this burgh and your tenants in the neighbourhood, do ourselves, as representing your ladyship's feuars here, the honour of presenting you with an address of welcome. On this, your ladyship's first public appearance in our town since the lamented death of your ladyship's late husband and son, we desire to express to you our sincere and heartfelt sympathy in your great sorrow and bereavement. In those noble Earls, your ladyship lost your nearest and dearest, and the feuars of Keith lost Superiors whom they honoured and loved and who had the best interests of Keith at their hearts. We congratulate your ladyship on the continued prosperity of the town. We have lately undertaken the carrying out of several necessary works, which will still further tend to beautify and improve the amenities of the burgh. We thank your ladyship for the great interest you have ever taken in matters affecting the town, and the readiness with which you have contributed materially and substantially to the well-being of the inhabitants. We humbly pray that your ladyship may long be spared to manage the large and important interests which have been committed to you. In name and on behalf of the Police Commissioners of Keith,

"T. A. Petrie Hay, chief magistrate."

The Countess of Seafield in reply said it was kind of the Commissioners to meet her that day. They would know and understand how she shrank from all public business, but she felt she could not refuse to receive them and accept this mark of their goodwill and their kindly welcome to the burgh of Keith. She should like to assure them that her great desire always was to continue the same kindly regard and the same earnest interest in their welfare that were felt by her husband and son for all on the estate. It did gratify her very deeply to hear from them that day how entirely the Commissioners appreciated the work they did, and she thanked them for those words and for their sympathy. She wished she could visit all the feuars and holders of land and make the acquaintance of their wives and families, but, as that was not possible, she must ask the Commissioners, as representing them, to be so good as to accept and convey to all her sincere good and kind wishes. It was a pleasure to congratulate Keith on being now a burgh, and with such an able Provost and body of Commissioners she felt assured Keith would continue to extend and prosper. They had always her best and heartiest wishes for their well-being and success. She thought she need hardly say that Mr Campbell was as anxious as she was to carry out all wise and useful improvements. She again thanked them for all they had said that day. The Countess afterwards, in company with Dr Campbell, visited a number of her tenantry in the vicinity of the town, and also the Institute and Hospital.

LADY SEAFIELD AND FISHING INTERESTS

The county of Banff stands supreme in Scotland in the number of its hardy and enterprising line fishermen, and on the Seafield estate there reside more of the class than perhaps on any other estate in Scotland. It was a fact of which Lady Seafield was proud, and in a manifold variety of ways she showed her abiding interest in the welfare of the fisheries There are Banff fishermen on the Seafield estate, Whitehills, Portsoy, Sandend, Cullen, Portknockie, Findochty, Portessie, Ianstown, are entirely upon the estate Lady Seafield saw many of these communities increase at a rate unprecedented in all their previous history. Since 1884 the whole of them have greatly enlarged their areas, and their assets in the form of fishing gear have increased in proportion Thirty years ago, Ianstown, so named after the eighth Earl, consisted of two or three houses; to-day it is one of the most populous centres in the growing town of Buckie In the harbour undertakings of the different communities Lady Seafield was a most generous friend Illustrations of the fact could be multiplied with ease, but as a case in point there may be taken the experiences of the Portsoy harbour undertaking At the last annual meeting of the shareholders of the harbour company there was submitted a statement of its financial history that cannot but to-day appeal to Lady Seafield's generous public spirit and to the liberal policy followed by those who preceded her in the administration of the great property The statement was in these terms.—

The harbour, the private property of Lord Seafield, was handed over by him to a public company under an Act of Parliament in 1882, for £6000. For this sum 600 shares of £10 each were allotted to Lord Seafield. Additional lands at Seatown and Links were, in 1883, purchased by the company from Lord Seafield for £1700 10s , per valuation of Mr Willet, C E. Of this sum £850 5s was paid to Lord Seafield in cash. The Company erected new buildings on the lands acquired of the value of £910 or thereby, bought up tenancy of houses for £160 and expended on roads and levelling lands £150 A loan of £2000 was procured from Alex. Raffan in 1883, and a bond was granted to Lord Seafield for £850 5s., being the balance of the price of lands. In 1889-90 Lady Seafield guaranteed a special advance of £6000 to the Union Bank and afterwards paid it off In 1910 Lady Seafield took over the bond due to the trustees of Alexander Raffan for £2000. Lady Seafield's interest was thus 600 shares at £10, £6000; loan over Seatown lands, £2850 5s ; advance paid to Union Bank, £6000; arrears of interests, £4221 0s 1d , being a total of £19,071 5s. 1d

At that meeting Dr Campbell, in referring to the statement and to the facts contained in it, remarked that he had acted in connection with the harbour personally for a period of about twenty-three years, and it would be within the recollection of his co-directors that when he first came to that county there was a balance due the bank of £6000. It was a question whether the then shareholders were not personally liable for that sum They were at their wits' end to know how to pay the balance due the bank. They failed to obtain money from any possible source and went to Lady Seafield She was kind enough to undertake to pay up that sum, and he supposed she had practically never received any interest for that sum Then only last year, when the Raffan Trustees called up their bond of £2000, Mr Young took every possible means to endeavour to get some other lender to take over the bond and keep the harbour going. But he failed to do so, and Mr Raffan's trustees took steps and arranged to advertise a portion of the harbour property, with a view of endeavouring to get sufficient funds to pay off the bond He did not think it would have been in the interests of Portsoy if the harbour had been allowed to become bankrupt, and it was to save that, and in the interests of the public of Portsoy, that Lady Seafield paid the £2000 and took over that bond. These were plain, simple facts which certainly made strong appeal to the intelligence and good sense of the community.

To go back a good few years anterior to that date, there may be recalled the opening by the Countess in 1900 of the fine new harbour at Portknockie, an undertaking that has proved of untold benefit to the interests of the enterprising community there. Lady Seafield was on that occasion happily described to the assembled fishermen as their natural, their best and most generous friend, and it was recalled how, in fulfilment of a promise made by her son, she had given to the scheme a contribution of £1000. At the opening on 25th April, her ladyship laid the memorial stone, and on that occasion made a happy little speech—

"I must first thank you all, friends, for so kindly wishing me to open this harbour, a harbour which will be of such untold usefulness, and which the most noble efforts of you Portknockie fishermen have so greatly helped to build My husband and son, as you well know, always took the deepest interest in your welfare, and, believe me, my feelings towards you will always be the same as theirs"

Lady Seafield was on the occasion presented with a silver trowel at the hands of Mr Joseph Mair, "Pim," and cheers were enthusiastically given for her ladyship. In the summer of the same year a project was under way for a new harbour at Whitehills, and here again her ladyship showed her warm and generous interest in her seafaring folks. She made a free gift to the community of the old harbour, also a site for the new harbour, and contributed £1000 to the building of the new harbour, handsome gifts which the villagers of Whitehills recall to-day with feelings of warm devotion and gratitude In May she visited the village in order to see the place, and the people, and the proposed site of the harbour Her ladyship delighted the fishermen and the women by the kindly enquiries she made, and the Countess was particularly gratified at the number of houses at whose windows there were bright and health-giving pot plants and flowers. She saw with interest the process of smoking haddocks and accepted a gift of some fish of the approved Whitehills cure. The Countess and party walked to Blackpots and the Red Well, and at the farm of the Old Manse saw a dwelling-house that had been finished there. On two later occasions her ladyship visited the village—to see the progress that was being made in the harbour works and again to see the completed structure In Sandend, too, where the material resources are small, the harbour was practically built through Lady Seafield's generosity, and naturally the welfare of the harbour of Cullen, which was presented to the community by Lord and Lady Seafield, was a matter that was very dear to her. To the Findochty harbour her ladyship and her husband also contributed over £1000, so that her interest in the numerous fishermen upon her estates and her warm care in their welfare were of the most generous and substantial kind.

RELIGIOUS AND PHILANTHROPIC WORK.

In the affairs of the Church of Scotland, Lady Seafield took a very great interest. We have seen how large was the ecclesiastical patronage that was exercised by successive Earls, and throughout the long life vouchsafed to her the Countess's practical help in matters affecting the Church was never invoked in vain. In her own Parish Church of Cullen, hallowed by the worship of centuries, and redolent of days that are distant, her interest was endless. To the neighbouring Church of Seafield she also displayed a thoughtful generosity. That church was erected in 1838 with little ornamentation, and, truth to tell, with small comfort to either minister or people. In 1887 it was reopened after undergoing renovation so extensive that its whole internal arrangements were altered and greatly improved. At that time the wish was expressed by members of the congregation to in some way commemorate Ian Charles, the eighth Earl, to whom they were chiefly indebted for the chapel of ease being erected into a *quoad sacra* parish in 1884. To that end a beautiful stained pictorial window was inserted in the building, comprising representations of the burning bush, figures of the apostles, &c., and representations also of fishes, a sheaf of corn, and the Seafield coat of arms, with appropriate texts. In lines extending along the top and bottom of the window, there is the inscription—" In loving memory of Ian Charles Ogilvie Grant, 8th Earl Seafield. Born 7th October 1851. Died 31st March 1884." No less in the churches on the Strathspey section of the estate did her ladyship display a warm generosity. Thus we find her in the autumn of 1805 opening a bazaar at Grantown held in aid of funds to increase the living of Inverallan Parish Church. On that occasion the Very Rev. Dr Donald Macleod of Glasgow spoke these tender words—

"This morning I visited for the first time that touching Memorial Church—I say touching Memorial Church, for I am certain that there is no one in Speyside but must heartily have sympathised with her upon whom the blow fell heaviest when she was deprived of the two greatest joys of her life, the father and the son. In God's mysterious providence, the young head of the Chief was laid low just at the time when his life was fullest of promise and of noblest thoughts for the good of the people and the good of the country. To this hour, I am sure, that the people of this district join with her in mourning the loss of those who were dear to her as her very life."

In the autumn of 1897 we find Lady Seafield laying the memorial stone of the Victoria Christian Institute at Grantown. Her ladyship was accompanied then by Lady Buchanan and the Hon. W. H. Gladstone, and pleasantly performing the little ceremony, she used these words—

"In thanking you for your wish that I should lay the memorial stone of the Christian Institute, I must assure you that I do so with very great pleasure, earnestly hoping that the building may prove a lasting happiness and encouragement to the young men and women of Strathspey for whom it is destined."

In August of the following year her ladyship opened a bazaar in aid of the building fund of the Institute and in doing so expressed her wish that "May God bless this pious undertaking." Then in August 1899 the Countess opened a bazaar at Grantown to increase the endowment of the parochial charge of Advie. Principal Story spoke on that occasion, and some words her ladyship used then may be recalled—

"It has given me much pleasure to accede to the invitation and the wishes of the minister and parishioners of Advie to open this bazaar which they have got up for the further endowment of the church of Advie. I am glad to join with them in thanking Principal Story for his kindness in coming to Strathspey to assist in this ceremony. I now declare the bazaar open, and I trust it may be a great success and answer the highest expectations of all interested in it."

In further illustration of her ladyship's boundless activity in all good works, it may be recalled how in August 1900 she opened a bazaar at Grantown in aid of the funds of the Baptist Church there—an organisation founded in 1805 as a result of a visit to the village, as it then was, of Mr J. A. Haldane. The Countess was on that occasion accompanied by Sir George Macpherson Grant. It was during an autumn visit to Castle Grant, too, that her ladyship unveiled the memorial to the late Professor Calderwood, of the Chair of Moral Philosophy in Edinburgh University, which finds a place in the Public Hall of Carr-Bridge. On that occasion Lady Seafield used these words—

"It gives me true pleasure to be permitted by the courtesy of the committee to show my great appreciation of Professor Calderwood's life and character by unveiling this tablet erected to his memory by the people of Duthil. We all know the increasing efforts, which with God's blessing I trust may not have been in vain, he made to promote their welfare, and we know how much his name will ever be loved and revered in this district. May I be allowed to express the heartfelt sorrow of Lady Buchanan and myself, in common with all here, for the loss we have sustained in the death of so good and so eminent a man, and our deep sympathy with Mrs Calderwood and her family."

The 1901 sale of work of the Women's Guild

of Cullen Parish Church was opened by her ladyship, and in the autumn of the following year she opened a sale of work at Grantown in aid of a fund for clearing off a debt incurred in repairs to the manse of Advie Then in the autumn of 1903 the Countess opened a sale of work organised by the congregation of Inverallan Parish Church in aid of the Church of Scotland's mission schemes, remarking then that

"I seem to have nothing to do but to thank you all for your kindly words and say what a pleasure it is to declare any good work like this open. May it be a great success."

Her ladyship performed a similar service at the Inverallan Church sale of work of 1905 On nearly every stall then could be found traces of her generosity, and one of the features of the principal stall was a large table cover of beautiful design, the work of her own hands On another occasion of a sale of work by the ladies' work party of the church of Inverallan, one of those who spoke was Sir Thomas M'Call Anderson, regius Professor of Medicine in Glasgow University. The Countess, after wishing the project all success, turned to Sir Thomas Anderson and said "I have to thank you, sir, for the pretty things you have said about Strathspey." These incidents are given only as examples of Lady Seafield's abounding interest in and endless work for religious and philanthropic organisations. They help to bring out in a measure her ladyship's firm and deep religious convictions, and show to some extent how anxious she was to play her part in the development and encouragement of all that affected the moral well-being of those on her estates That was a feature of her lovely character that will with many be a pleasant memory for long.

A GRACIOUS HOSTESS.

Lady Seafield on various occasions was the gracious hostess of members of the Royal Family. We have seen the terms of friendship on which her son was with the Duke of Albany, and from time to time visits were paid by members of the Royal Family both to Castle Grant and Cullen House. Those who had the privilege of attending the Diamond Jubilee celebrations at Cullen of Queen Victoria will not soon forget the feeling and tender words then spoken by the Countess. A great procession had been formed on the Square of the burgh, and marching to Cullen House, Lady Seafield appeared at the main entrance, and facing the cheering crowd of her neighbours of Cullen and district, she said—

"Gentlemen, I have to thank you all, the burghers and others of Cullen, in again kindly giving me the opportunity of joining you in these national demonstrations. We, together with all loyal subjects of Great Britain and its Dependencies, have never had such cause for rejoicing as we have to-day through the goodness of God in having given us for sixty years such a great and noble woman as Queen Victoria to rule this mighty Empire. We may well indeed all join in thanking Him for His gracious love and care of our country and in praying Him to spare her for many years. God bless our dear Queen and Empress."

On his annual shooting visits to Tulchan, the Prince of Wales—later, His Majesty King Edward — always spent a day or days on the extensive moors of Castle Grant, and His Royal Highness always, when her ladyship was then in residence, visited her. His Majesty likewise visited Castle Grant, and in the autumn of 1909, which the Countess spent at Cullen House, feeling unable for the exertions of a stay at her Highland home, the King honoured her ladyship with a visit. It took place on September 16, and the occasion, we are sure, is still fresh in the minds of hundreds of readers who had then the privilege of seeing His Majesty proceed through Cullen and some of the picturesque and prosperous fishing villages on the coast of Rathven. A month later the Prince of Wales, now His Majesty King George, then the guest of the Duke of Richmond and Gordon, also travelled to Cullen House to visit the Countess In this connection there may be recalled the visit of Lord Rosebery to Cullen House in January 1909 His lordship was Lady Seafield's guest over a Sunday, on which day both the Countess and the ex-Premier attended service in the very old and historic parish church When his lordship left the following afternoon there was quite a demonstration at the station, and in reply to words of welcome and farewell, Lord Rosebery expressed the pleasure it had given him to pay Lady Seafield a visit at Cullen House. Her ladyship, he said, was known far and near as a beneficent proprietrix, who had devoted her life to the interests of the tenants and communities on her large estates, and he congratulated the Council and town on having so excellent a Superior in their near neighbourhood.

LADY SEAFIELD AND THE SERVICES.

From her position and family connections the Countess of Seafield took naturally a great and abiding interest in the country's defences, and she showed it in many practical ways When in August 1900 a bazaar was opened at Cullen by the Duke of Fife in aid of the local Volunteer organisation, the Countess accompanied His Grace from Cullen House to the hall in which the gathering was held, and the Duke in his remarks on that occasion said.

"It is very gratifying to me, as I am sure it must be to you, to see present to-day amongst us one who is so universally respected and beloved, not only in Cullen but throughout the North. I need hardly say that I allude to Lady Seafield who has so kindly accompanied me here to-day."

In October of the following year, when the members of the Elginshire contingent of the Volunteer Service Company were, at Elgin, presented with medals for service in the South African War, the ceremony was performed by the Countess of Seafield, who on that occasion said—

"I have been requested to perform this ceremony, and I have very great pleasure in coming and presenting these well earned medals to the brave men who so willingly volunteered to serve their country in South Africa I am proud to think that our country has sent so many Moray loons as a contingent to our illustrious army You have done your duty gallantly, and we thank you with full hearts While doing so, let us never forget your brave and noble comrades who have laid down their lives in that distant land, leaving a grand example of devotion and of loyalty to their home and country"

With a winning smile and a kindly word to each, her ladyship pinned the medal on the left breast of each soldier and warmly shook hands with him at parting. In June 1905 the Countess entertained at Cullen House the Banffshire contingent of the Scottish Horse on their return home from their annual training at camp at Dunkeld. On that occasion Dr Campbell, speaking on behalf of Lady Seafield, said her ladyship was very glad to see them all back safely from their arduous training among the Perthshire mountains, and was pleased that Banffshire had sent such a good representation for the service of the country. Then in August 1906, when that famous regiment, the London Scottish, had a route march in the Highlands, they were bountifully entertained at Carr-Bridge by the Countess. To the last her ladyship's interest in the Services and in everything that tended to their wellbeing and efficiency was very great. They had in her a true and influential friend.

CHIEFTAINESS OF CLAN GRANT.

Lady Seafield occupied the proud position of Chieftainess of the Clan Grant, and in the autumn of 1898 she had the happiness of welcoming to Castle Grant the members of the clan on their annual reunion at their headquarters in the Highlands. From Strathspey, Glasgow, and elsewhere, there was a great gathering of the clansmen who marched in procession from the Square of Grantown to the Castle, where they were the guests of her ladyship. The toast of the Chieftainess of the Clan was proposed in eloquent words by Sir George Macpherson Grant—

"Lady Seafield has been long connected with Strathspey, and during that time she has well and worthily maintained the traditions of the great House of Grant. By her generous and considerate treatment of her tenantry on her vast estates, she has secured their respect and she has secured their goodwill. I go further than that and I say that by many acts of kindness and many acts of consideration, she has proved to be a worthy member of the clan Grant, and she has secured the devoted friendship and attachment of every man and woman of it. Lady Seafield has won the hearts of all around her, and my Lady, you will pardon me when I say on this occasion that there are none who have sympathised with you in your sorrows more than the men and women you see before you. He who will not drain his glass and drink to the long life and health of our worthy hostess surely is not fit to be a Grant."

The Chieftainess in her reply said—

"I thank you from my heart. And now before we part I wish to propose with all my heart the health, prosperity and welfare of our grand old Clan Grant."

SOME PUBLIC ACTIVITIES.

In the more or less public business of the wide district which was proud to have the Countess of Seafield as its Superior, her ladyship took from time to time an active and interesting part. It was she, for instance, who in 1899 opened the new bridge across the Spey at Boat of Garten. In a lovely day of August in that year, her ladyship, amid a large concourse of people, went to the centre of the bridge and there with a mallet finished the driving of the last nail in the bridge, thus completing the structure. Then, at the Duthil side, she cut with a scissors a ribbon that was extended across the bridge, and in a few happy remarks expressed the wish that it might prove a great convenience to the district and promote the comfort and prosperity of the residents. In the autumn of 1902, the Countess opened a bazaar at Cullen held in aid of the funds of the bowling green and tennis court, saying on that occasion,

"I have very great pleasure in doing what the Provost and committee asked me to do. I wish this bazaar every success, and I sincerely trust that the object of the bazaar, which the promoters have so much at heart, may not only prove a source of amusement but of great benefit to everyone and to all classes in the district."

Three weeks later, her ladyship opened a

bazaar at Grantown held to provide a club-house and showyard fittings for the old-established Strathspey Farmer Club It was a matter, as affecting the well-being of her Speyside farming tenants, in which Lady Seafield took a great interest, as may be gathered from the words she then spoke—

"It is a great privilege, and a privilege I am particularly proud of, to be able to help in any way the farming industry of Strathspey for the farmers have often to contend with late seasons; so with great goodwill I declare the bazaar open and wish it all success."

Then in August of the following year the Countess drove from Castle Grant to Rothes, and there opened a bazaar for the purpose of raising funds to wipe off a debt of over £800 incurred in the building of the Town Hall On that occasion her ladyship, before leaving, handed to the Provost a handsome sum of money for behoof of the poor of the parish The most important of Lady Seafield's later appearances in a public capacity, however, was in July 1904, when she opened the hospital at Portsoy for infectious diseases provided through the munificent generosity of Dr Campbell, Convener of the County of Banff, for the district of Lower Banffshire There was a great gathering on the occasion and there were many interesting speeches The remarks of Lady Seafield on the occasion were very pleasant—

"The Board of the Campbell Hospital for infectious cases have given me much pleasure in asking me to declare open this hospital, the munificent gift of Dr Campbell, for which we can never sufficiently thank the generous donor. Without Dr Campbell's aid, it would have been long ere Lower Banffshire could have borne so heavy a cost. Not only has Dr Campbell provided the funds, but we must also remember the brain-work he has given to make the building he presents to you as perfect as you now see—so perfect that now and in future generations it will be a priceless boon not only for the sick but also to the public by the means it gives for isolating infection. I am very certain that all here and in Lower Banffshire would wish me to thank Dr Campbell, but I fear I have no words to properly express such a volume of thanks. I know that I am one of the most grateful recipients of his princely gift."

Lady Seafield then advanced to the main door of the administrative block, and turning the handle of the door and pushing it open said—"In the name of God the Father, God the Son, and God the Holy Ghost, I declare open the Campbell Infectious Hospital. May God bless its work and its donor." At the close of the opening ceremony, the Countess called for three cheers for Dr Campbell, herself leading off the demonstration by waving her hand.

Lady Seafield took the keenest possible interest in educational affairs. As the erstwhile patron of bursaries that have been of untold benefit in the lives of very many, her interest was particularly keen in the ancient seat of learning in the village of Fordyce at which they were held, and matters affecting its welfare were very near her heart. To ensure its continued prosperity her ladyship expended time and thought and money, and the institution ever had in her the warmest of friends. It may be recalled, too, how in 1903 she presented the prizes to pupils at the school of Cullen, when Dr Campbell, in acknowledging a vote of thanks to her ladyship, said Lady Seafield was very much gratified by what she had seen and heard that day, and she had authorised him to state that as a slight expression of her appreciation of the excellent work carried on by the teachers and pupils of the school and also in respect of her own great interest in that old school and the good old town of Cullen, with their approval, she wished to contribute to the school prize fund for next year a sum of seven guineas. Then in a word it may be recalled how, two years later, youthful members of the Cullen Boys' Brigade spent a happy autumn day as the guests of the Countess at Castle Grant. We may recall, too, how, by her ladyship's thoughtful kindness, the people of Cullen and district, on the first day of 1909, enjoyed a series of pleasant entertainments, which made that New Year's Day one of the happiest they had experienced for long. Lady Seafield was herself present at an afternoon entertainment for children and at the earlier of two evening performances. On Empire Day in 1909 the children of Cullen spent a very happy afternoon at Cullen House as the guests of her ladyship.

As the owner of a large estate the Countess of Seafield herself showed a brilliant example in the farming of land and in the cultivation of farm live stock of the highest class. At Cullen House her ladyship maintained one of the finest herds in the country of Aberdeen-Angus cattle. Members of it have won worldwide honours, and animals drawn from it have gone to enrich many collections of the breed, both in this country and in the United States. She followed the fortunes of her favourites in the showyard with much interest, and naturally she was very proud when at the Smithfield show of 1908 an animal bred and fed at Cullen House won the blue ribbon of the fat stock shows of the Kingdom. At the summer shows, too, members of the herd have won the highest distinctions. At Castle Grant her ladyship maintained a large and valuable fold of the picturesque Highland breed. It also has been most successful, and the lines of breeding represented in it are held in high appreciation by patrons of the variety.

Perhaps in no more distinctive way did Lady Seafield's beautiful womanly qualities find expression than in founding and carrying on the Clothing Club that is associated with her name. Branches of it are to be found all over the estate, and the good it has done can never be computed. The large subscriptions which she added to those of its individual members were of great immediate benefit, but not less valuable was the spirit it fostered of a splendid independence and the encouragement it gave to household economy and thrift. It is an institution by which hundreds of poor families have been materially helped in their journey through life, and they will recall it with affection and gratitude to-day when their noble benefactor has passed from amongst them.

For many years the Countess of Seafield had the comforting presence and loved society of her widowed sister Lady Buchanan, and her death, which took place at Castle Grant on 21st March 1904, was a great blow to her. Lady Buchanan was widow of Sir Andrew Buchanan, G C B, who had a long and brilliant diplomatic career. She was married in 1859, and accompanied her husband to The Hague, Berlin, St Petersburg, and Vienna, at each of which capitals he was in succession Ambassador for Great Britain. During the heavy family affliction that overtook the Countess of Seafield, Lady Buchanan proved of the greatest service by her sympathetic and wise counsel. She possessed in a notable degree, with a sweet and dignified manner, the family strength of character. The bond of affection between the two sisters was very strong, and Lady Seafield felt the death of Lady Buchanan keenly.

Thus did the Countess of Seafield touch life's activities at many points. To a woman's sym pathy and capacity of tender affection she added a courage that was rare and an aptitude for work that is not common For over a quarter of a century she had the administration of one of the greatest landed properties in the North—a property on which there are vast interests represented by cultivators of the soil, tradesmen, workers, and those who find their livelihood on the deep. With the aspirations of each and every class she could deeply sympathise, and nothing was ever wanting on her part to allow them to be realised Her tender winning ways, her musical voice, the slight and gentle figure in the widow's weeds, her great natural gifts of sympathy, her attractive manner and her high-souled and lovely character will not soon be forgotten, and with these there will always likewise be borne in affectionate and respectful admiration her comprehensive grasp of business, her enlightened management of the great trust committed to her care, her fine courage under the most cruel of sorrows, and the arduous life she led while health and strength were given her For many a year to come "Lady Seafield" will, in the North, mean the noble Countess who has just passed to her rest

---

The "Times" of Saturday, in a notice of Lady Seafield's life, remarks that during the Dowager Countess's tenure of 25 years the administration of the property has been admirable, and every function of a great landlord splendidly performed. Lovers of art owe her a debt of gratitude, for in the churches of Cullen and Deskford she, as sole "heritor," preserved two splendid stone sacramentaries, architectural ornaments probably not to be found in any other building occupied by Presbyterians. It is, however, by their afforestation that the recent Earls and late Countess will be best remembered Lady Seafield was the greatest owner of woodlands in the United Kingdom.

It is computed that the number of pine trees planted by her husband, her son, and herself amounted to 50,000,000 in Strathspey and Aviemore alone The proprietors were fortunate in their manager, Mr Grant Thomson, who has done so much to advance the science of forestry, but without such a landlord his vast experience could not have been acquired. In the Transactions of the Royal Scottish Arboricultural Society—especially those for 1894 and 1907—may be found particulars of deep interest relating to the management of the Seafield estates and the art of forestry there taught. The cost of planting 80 years ago was about 50s an acre, when wages were 7s. a week and seedlings one-fifth of their present price. It is now, of course, much greater. No man advanced in life can undertake such work without sinking a great capital, which will yield him little or nothing in his lifetime. As one who worthily filled a distinguished situation in the social system now passing away, Lady Seafield will be long remembered with affection and respect

THE FUNERAL.

IMPOSING CEREMONIES.

After a series of ceremonials, stately and appealing in their very simplicity, accompanied by that natural grandeur that is ever associated with human sympathy and emotion that are deeply felt, and that in this instance were vouchsafed in full and overflowing measure, the Right Honourable Caroline Countess Dowager of Seafield now sleeps in the mausoleum of the ancient and historic House of Grant, at Duthil, away in the heart of the hills where is still the territorial stronghold of the powerful clan At Cullen and at Grantown, at the peaceful hamlet at Duthil also, nestling in the great pinewoods of Strathspey, the proceedings were on a scale and were of a nature that will never be forgotten by the thousands of people who were present at one or other of the appealing and affecting ceremonies. Lady Seafield, loved and honoured in life, held in the highest regard and deepest affection, went to her last home amid a signal and remarkable outpouring of the feelings of respectful admiration that she had ever evoked, and in not a few cases too amid the tears of sincere mourners. The ceremonies, lasting as they did over two days, and in scene divided by many miles of fertile plain and expanses of hill and heather and forest, extending from sea-washed shore to the Central Highlands were taken part in by a very great number of all those numerous people of the North of Scotland whose proud privilege it had been to bestow upon her the name of Superior or of Chieftainess, and with everyone who saw them they will remain an abiding memory. Let two little incidents, slight they were but very significant, suffice to illustrate in a measure the feeling that throughout these north-eastern parts was universal The coffin in which the remains rested had been carried from the hall of Cullen House to a short distance beyond the doorway, where the funeral service was conducted. Round about, in a semi-circle, stood perhaps two thousand mourners. The brilliant sunshine of a lovely October morning was radiating as though with colours of gold the fading leaves of the fine old trees around the stately House And then, from amidst the vast throng, there stepped an elderly man, a farmer he seemed Hard physical work he had probably known, for his shoulders were bent, and he leant on his staff for support. He walked up to the coffin, unhindered by anyone, for the sentiment in his heart was easily seen, and he was representative of a class in whose welfare the Countess had ever been interested. Slowly with his ageing eyes he read the inscription on the coffin Then he walked away, back to the ranks of the mourners And one who was near him heard the sob he gave, saw the handkerchief drawn out—we need say no more At the close of the service something similar took place, and in this case it recalled in a picturesque and tender way the abiding and bountiful interest which Lady Seafield took in those flourishing and increasing communities that line the seaboard at the northern boundary of the great estate. Three women, with black shawls over their heads, who had been standing in the background sorrowfully watching the proceedings, made some efforts to approach the coffin. In a kindly word they were at once invited to come forward by one of the chief mourners, and the three fisher women, in their humble, but none the less eloquent mourning attire, paid their tribute of sorrow and devotion by the side of the coffin which contained the remains of a lady whose heart had ever turned fondly to her fisher folks Such simple and beautiful little acts, done naturally and quietly, and with a sincerity that was manifest, seemed to strike with peculiar force the true note of the occasion—an exalted lady going down to her grave with the accompaniment of the tears and the laments of great sorrowing communities for whose welfare she had ever striven.

At Cullen House.

This feeling of close association with the people among whom she lived was further emphasised by proceedings that preceded the removal of the body On Tuesday the remains lay in state in the spacious hall of Cullen House. The coffin rested on trestles and was covered with a pall of dress Grant tartan; on the top was a single cross of blue flowers, the tribute of Sir David and Lady and Miss Baird, and all around the apartment were lovely masses of wreaths and flowers that had been sent by sorrowing relatives and friends The coffin was of panelled and polished oak enclosing a lead shell, and on it was a brass plate with the inscription—

Caroline Stuart,
Countess of Seafield
Born
30th June, 1830
Died
6th October, 1911.

On Tuesday numerous residents in the district, from Cullen, Portknockie, Deskford, and farther afield, paid their last personal tribute of affection and respect to the venerable and venerated lady, who for more than sixty years had been intimately associated with them and their interests

On Wednesday the first stage of the journey was accomplished—from the principal seat of the family at Cullen House to their Highland

seat at Castle Grant, in storied Strathspey.
The day broke dull and cloudy Heavy
banks reduced the area of the physical outlook, but by ten o'clock the sun had pierced
its way through the haze and all day long it
shone with a power that for mid-October was
even brilliant In the lovely demesne, the
leaves of the trees were yellowing unto winter,
and reflected back as though by burnished
sheen the gleams of the welcome sun The
town of Cullen had the sombre appearance that
befitted the solemn occasion. It was a town
and a community of mourning such as has not
been often experienced in all the many years
of its burghal history. Places of business were
closed for practically the whole day The
town's flag was flying at half mast, and the
tolling of the town's bell mingled with that
of the bell of the ancient and picturesque
church of the parish to proclaim in an audible
way the sorrow which filled the minds and
hearts of all Blinds in houses and shops
were drawn, movement through the streets
was made in a quiet and chastened way—it
was a silent town seen on a day that was devoted to mourning The morning trains
brought to the burgh vast numbers of people.
Many came by road, and there were numerous
motors and ten o'clock had not long passed
ere the avenue to the House was occupied by
successive crowds of people, attired in dress
of deep mourning, on their way through the
lovely woods of the policies to the stately
mansion house that had been bereft of its aged
mistress. The soft green lawns, the sun-kissed
tints of mellowing autumn, the stately old
trees, the fine pile of the House itself, and
the prattling waters of the burn as they danced
on to the sea made a fitting setting for the
solemn ceremony that was about to take place,
and the mournful tolling of the bell of a church
whose associations tradition has connected

with Robert the Bruce as it sounded over the trees and through the glades and down to the valleys added to the silent solemnity that marked the tone and was indeed itself the tone of the whole moving proceedings. Before the coffin was removed from the hall, many hundreds of mourners passed through it to pay a last tribute of esteem and regard. By eleven o'clock there had gathered in the vicinity of the House people to the number perhaps of two thousand, and they included not a few ladies dressed in deepest black and a good few also of the local fishing community whose black shawls and skirts were their humble and heartfelt visible evidences of mourning. To the left of the House were gathered representatives of many public bodies; to the right was the large body of tenantry and of the general public who had come from over a wide area of the North Then a few minutes past eleven, the coffin was carried out of the House and placed in the centre between the two long lines that extended from the doorway right across the lawn. It rested on trestles, and over it was the pall of the clan tartan and the cross of lovely blue flowers There took up a position at the head of the coffin—Rev James M'Intyre, Seafield; Rev. W. G G. M'Lean, Cullen Parish Church; and Rev. G. M Park, Deskford Parish Church. At hand, the chief mourners assembled—the Earl of Seafield; the Earl of Cassillis, a grand-nephew, and Lady Cassillis; Captain David Baird, M V O., and Mr William Baird of Erskine, grand-nephews, Sir John Innes, Bart, of Edingight, Miss Innes, Sir George Abercromby, Bart, of Forglen, Captain Abercromby, with Mr James Campbell, D.L., LL.D , commissioner for Lady Seafield; Mrs Campbell, Mr E. J Cuthbertson, W S , Edinburgh; Mr D T Samson, factor, Elgin; and Mr Garden of Troup Just at hand also there stood Mr W.

MacIntosh, Fife Lodge, Banff, representing His Grace the Duke of Fife, K G., K.T., and Mr Ranald R Macdonald, Cluny, representing Lady Gordon Cathcart of Cluny. Near the doorway there also stood the house servants, male and female, a mournful company, among them Nurse Watson who had devotedly attended Lady Seafield in her later years At hand also were estate employes, mourning the death of a loved and venerated mistress In front was the great band of mourners, standing bareheaded, and taking part in the service with feelings of reverential devotion All the while the solemn knell of the bell of the parish church, situated quite near the House, sounded aloud something of the sorrow that was felt by all

The service was begun by Mr M'Lean, who, in a voice that reached all of the vast company, recited the lines —

In the midst of life we are in death. Of whom may we seek for succour but of Thee, O Lord, in whom our souls do rest and hope.

I am the Resurection and the Life, saith the Lord, he that believeth in Me, though he were dead, yet shall he live, and whosoever liveth and believeth in Me shall never die

Then Mr M'Intyre read the Scripture lessons The first was from Psalm ciii.—"The Lord is merciful and gracious, slow to anger, and plenteous in mercy He will not always chide; neither will he keep his anger for ever." The second was from St John xiv.—"Let not your heart be troubled; ye believe in God, believe also in me In my Father's house are many mansions; if it were not so, I would have told you I go to prepare a place for you. And if I go and prepare a place for you, I will come again, and receive you unto myself, that where I am, there ye may be also." The last lesson Mr M'Intyre read was from Revelation vii.— "After this I beheld, and, lo, a great multitude which no man could number, of all nations, and kindreds, and people, and tongues, stood before the throne, and before the Lamb, clothed with white robes, and palms in their hands; And cried with a loud voice saying, Salvation to our God, which sitteth upon the throne, and unto the Lamb" Then Mr M'Lean led in prayer as follows —

Almighty and everlasting God, who sendest forth Thy Spirit and we are created, and who takest away our breath and we die and return to dust, we bow before Thee with reverence and deep humility under the shadow of a great sorrow It is only when Thou takest away that we realise how much Thou hast given We thank Thee for the saintly life of Thy servant who now rests from her earthly labours and has entered upon the higher service of those who, through faith, inherit the promises. We rejoice that she filled with so much grace and acceptance the high social position she occupied, and we thank Thee for the beautiful life she lived, for her sympathy with the sad, the poor, and the suffering, for her generous benefactions, for her life-long interest in her tenantry, for her many womanly virtues and for the example she has left us by the unfailing regularity with which, along with her own people, she worshipped here in Thy holy house. Heavy was the cross Thou didst lay upon her—we thank Thee for the grace which enabled her to bear it patiently and bravely through many weary years, for that true communion of spirit which was hers with the dear departed, for her loving trust in Thee "through life's long day and death's dark night," and that at eventide she entered the valley of the shadow, leaning upon her Beloved and fearing no evil. For the example of a life in the beauty and nobility of which we rejoiced, and for the end of which we now sorrow, we praise and bless Thy holy name. We would keep ever clear and bright the sweet memory of her saintly life to cheer and help us on our way. Father of mercies and God of all comfort we remember before Thee those upon whom the blow has fallen most heavily, praying that they may be sustained by the joyful expectation of meeting again with the loved ones who have gone before, and being joined with them in still closer and dearer bonds of love and holy service. Sanctify to all of us this solemn dispensation of Thy providence, and as we, with sad hearts, follow the remains of our dear departed sister to their last long resting-place, do Thou comfort us with those blessed hopes which no earthly trouble or sorrow can overshadow. "Father, in Thy gracious keeping, leave we now Thy servant sleeping, until the Day dawn and the shadows have for ever passed away" Through Jesus Christ, Our Lord, Amen.

Then Mr Park pronounced the benediction, and the brief and beautiful service ended.

Then a great procession was marshalled in the following order—(1) Town Council of Cullen and Town's Officer with draped halberd; other Public Bodies following; (2) Estate Employes; (3) Funeral Car; (4) Lady Seafield's Empty Carriage, (5) Car with Wreaths, (6) Mourning Coaches, (7) General Public, walking four deep, (8) Horse Conveyances, (9) Motors. The funeral car was drawn by four handsome black horses Lady Seafield's empty carriage, which immediately followed, with blinds closely drawn, was to many an affecting sight; it was drawn by two beautiful black horses, driven by her ladyship's devoted coachman, Mr Nicholson. The car with the wreaths was the cynosure of many mourning eyes, proclaiming as these did in this pure and beautiful form, the love and affection of many friends. In the mourning coaches the chief mourners were accommodated, although some of them took part in the procession on foot. The attendance of the public and of representatives of public bodies was very great, and the whole formed an imposing spectacle as in long array it was drawn up in the avenue leading from Cullen House. Then, when all things were ready, the order to march was given by Mr Hope, chief constable, and with slow and measured step a vast company of mourners attended Lady Seafield in her last journey from her beautiful and much loved home. The notes of the church bell continued their solemn peals and wafted up among the trees came the sounds of the bell in the burgh. Little groups of women, some of them tear-stained, saw the great body of people pass while they stood in the shelter of spreading trees. At Cullen, where business activities of all kinds had been for some time suspended, there were crowds of people at every corner. The Square was crowded, the steps in front of the Town Hall were occupied to their extreme limit, and, looking up Seafield Street, there was a sea of faces, very many of them those of school children, who lined the roadway for a long distance up. Just at noon the funeral car passed the town's clock. Then to the left the procession went by the foot of the school playground, and, turning again, proceeded along Reidhaven Street to the station yard. Throughout its progress in the burgh, the spectacle was of a moving kind, one that appealed strongly to human emotions, and if these in many cases could not be restrained, it was but an evidence of the strong pent-up feelings held so strongly that they could not do otherwise than find expression. Through all the streets to that solemn burden in the funeral car loving homage was done, and when at length the station was reached, there were further manifestations of sympathetic feeling. Quietly and quickly the coffin was removed to a saloon forming part of a special train that was standing in readiness at the platform; the many floral tributes of love and devotion were entrained; the chief mourners took their seats, and in a few minutes, with every head unbared of those who stood on the platform and who crowded the station approaches, the train glided silently away, over the viaduct, over the embankment that looks down upon Cullen's links and sandy shores, through the wholly Seafield villages of Portknockie, Findochty, Portessie, and Ianstown, away by Elgin and Forres to Castle Grant. The Countess had left her beautiful home by the shores of the Moray Firth for ever.

To give a list of all those present would be to attempt an impossible task. We can hope only to give some, and these may be taken as typical of the many classes of people who took part in this great and affecting ceremony. We may begin perhaps with the public boards, many of which were officially represented. Leading the procession was Cullen Town Council, whose members were preceded by their halbardier, Mr John Simpson, carrying a halberd, which was heavily draped, and were accompanied by Mr W. C. Paterson, town clerk, and Mr W. W. Walker, town chamberlain. There was a full representation of the Council, and there were present also representatives of the Cullen School Board, the Cullen Parish Council, and the Cullen Harbour Board. The Provost, magistrates, and Town Council of Banff were also present, the Provost wearing his chain of office. They were preceded by Mr P. Hutcheon, who carried a heavily draped halberd, and were accompanied by Mr James Grant, town and county clerk; Mr P Stewart, town clerk depute, and Mr R. Stuart, burgh surveyor. The magistrates and Town Council of Portsoy had also a large representation; they were accompanied by Mr James Young, town clerk, and Mr W. Ingram, procurator-fiscal, and clerk of Fordyce School Board. Other bodies represented by members or officials or both were the Boyndie, Banff, Rathven, Deskford, Fordyce, and other Parish Councils, the School Boards of these places, and other statutory bodies in the northeast, the names of many of their representatives being mentioned below. The Aberdeen

University Court was represented by Professor Cowan, D.D., Aberdeen, and the Great North Railway Company by Mr Deuchar, passenger superintendent. Among others observed were—

Sheriff Dudley Stuart, Banff; Mr Davidson, York House, Cullen, Major Chinn, Portsoy; Mr Alex. Colville, solicitor, Banff; Dr Fergusson. Banff; Mr Wm. Forbes, Cowhythe, chairman of Fordyce School Board; Mr R. G. Shirreffs, sheriff clerk of Banffshire, Mr R. Y. Mackay, procurator fiscal of Banffshire; Mr Sharpe, assistant factor, Cullen House; Mr L Beaton, farm manager, Cullen House, Rev. Dr Bruce, Banff; Rev. James G Ledingham, Boyndie; Rev. A. Johnston, Grange; Rev. John Southby, Portsoy; Rev. A. M. Gibson, do ; Rev. C. J. Davidson, do , Rev. J C MacGregor, Fordyce; Rev. George Grant, Ord; Rev Lithgow Wilson, Cullen; Rev James Robertson, Fordyce; Rev. Hugh Fitzpatrick, Keith; Rev Wm Simmers, Portsoy, Rev. Dr Miller, Buckie, chairman of Rathven School Board, Rev. Sydney Smith, Keith; Rev. Mr Howie, Enzie; Rev. John L. Symington, Rathven; Rev. John Graham, Buckie; Rev Mr M'Kee, Findochty; Rev. James Morrison, Deskford, Rev J. Greenlaw, Buckie; Rev. W. Morton, Buckie; Charles Wilson, station agent, Cullen; Wm Maclennan, Bogton; James Cruickshank, Portsoy, Geo Mitchell, Midtown; John Watt, Blairmaud; Chas. Wilson, Portsoy; Alex. M. Ogilvie, Tillynaught; Fortune Ogilvie, Tillynaught; J. Muiry, Baronsmill; Alex. Anderson, Drakemyres, J. K. Anderson, bank agent, Portsoy; Alex Baillie, Portsoy, R. Gray, Arnbath; Alex. M'Connachie, do.; James Maclennan, Redhythe; W. H. Hartley, Portsoy, G G. M'Robie, Portsoy; W. Sievwright, Reidside; A. M'Connachie, Baley; John M'Intyre, Portsoy; John Gillan, do.; A. O. Scrimgeour, do ; Captain L. Jack, do.; John Bennett, Redstack; George Thomson, Kindrought; D. O. Stevenson, Mains of Durn; George Christie, The Brae, George Christie, jun., do.; A. Simpson, schoolmaster, Portsoy; Alexander Lyon, Brangan; John Fortune, Smiddyboyne; William Turner, Cairnton; Jas Dawson, Tillynaught; Alexander Munro,

Cairns; James Barclay Aulton; Alexander Forbes, Rettie; George Smith, Ordens, chairman of Boyndie School Board; Alexander Smith, Thriepland; Alexander Allan, Baldavie; Robert Wyllie, banker, Banff, George Imlach, Wyllieholes; Ex-Provost Alexander, Banff, Ex-Provost Munro, Banff, Ex-Provost Lyon, Banff; Mr John A Badenoch, clerk, Banff Burgh School Board; Charles Cosser, Parish Council Clerk, Banff; George Findlay, retired merchant, Whitehills; Alex. Murray, chairman, Boyndie Parish Council; James G Murray, Whitehills, Dr Ledingham, medical officer of Banffshire; J M Ewan, Auds, Henry Watson, baker, Whitehills, Alex. Still, clerk to the Parish Council and School Board of Boyndie; George Cooper, Greenriggs, Fordyce, J Smith, Auchnaggatt, for many years head gardener at Cullen House; Alexander Brodie, solicitor, Banff, Jas. Gray, hotel keeper, Whitehills, W Hay, Portsoy, Alexander Horne, Bogierow; George Low, Highfield, A Donald, Portsoy, James Hay, Sandend; William Smith, do; James Wright, Boyne Mills; John Mackay, Mill of Tillynaught; John Gordon, Burnside, James Smith, Williamston, Fraser, Bogmuchals, Fraser, Culphin Toll Bar, Hepburn, Wellhead; George Anderson Simpson, headmaster, Fordyce Academy; Stewart, Hillend, Ward, Keith, Ex-Provost Burgess Portsoy, representing Portsoy Harbour Board, Ex-Provost Clark. Portsoy; James Mackintosh, county sanitary inspector, Banff; Wm Taylor, Begburn, J. Wiseman, Mains of Badenyouchers; A. Findlater, Brodiesord; Wm. Thompson, Post Office Fordyce, James Forbes, Hallyard, Theodore Chalmers, Fordyce, G. Davidson, Drochedlie; Wm. Bremner, Hopetoun, John W. Gordon, Inspector of Poor for Rathven; Alex. Cumming, Muir of Rettie; J Macdonald, Ordens; Wm. Donald, Kirkhill, John Fordyce, Rosebank, John Green, Duffushillock, R. Cruickshank, Inspector of Poor, Deskford; John Lobban, Denside, Seafield, J. Gray, Knowes, Desk-W. Stevenson, Carestown, James Maitland, Raemore, Deskford; W. Sutherland, Mains of Findochty, A Cheyne, Cullen; J. F. Cheyne, do.; H. L. Cheyne, do.; J. F. Grant, Square,

Cullen; A. Hendry, Sheriffseat, Ord; John Davidson, Shannelton, Ord; A. Smith, Upper Culphin; James Stewart, Hillend, Fordyce; A Mair, "Big," fisherman, Portknockie; Donald Schoolhouse, Portknockie, Wilson, Schoolhouse, Whitehills, Scott, Schoolhouse, Deskford, A. Mitchell, Cullen, John Forbes, Cullen; George Robertson, do., W. Paterson, Portsoy; A. Milne, Burnsford, Deskford, George Mitchell, Durn House; Robertson, draper, Cullen; W. May, Cullen, W. Wilson, Warylip; G. W. Clark, Cullen, J. Dunbar, do ; J Simpson, do ; Arthur Duffus, T Buttress, R Newton (of Messrs Newton Bros., Cullen), Cowie, Inaltrie, Deskford; M'Connachie, Ardoch, Stewart, Nether Blairock; Kitchen, Clune, Morrison, Clunehill; Simpson, dairyman, Banff; Findlay, jun , merchant, Whitehills; Mackessack, auctioneer, Banff; Alex. Morrison, Loanhead; Morrison, White Culphin, Macpherson, Auchmillie, Jas. Reid, Cullen, H. J Napier, Boyndie; Wilson, Burns; Dr Galloway, Banff, Dr M'Hardy, Cullen; John L M'Naughton, town clerk of Buckie; Provost Archibald, Buckie; George Garden, Rannachie; James Wood, Cullen; Forbes, Dallachie, A. T. Garden, Brankanentham; Yuill, Schoolhouse, Findochty, Gunn, Kilnhillock; Wm. Wilson, Tochineal, J W. Gordon, Inspector of Poor, Cullen; Dr Duguid, Buckie, John Barclay, chairman of Rathven Parish Council, Blacklaws, Portsoy; Christie, Roseacre, John Dawson, Buckie; Peter Cowie, "Busie," Portessie; T. J Anderson, bank agent, Buckie; Jamieson, Mains of Skeith; A. G Retti, Ceylon; L. Milne, Rannas, J. Donaldson, Portknockie; Alex. Gordon, bank agent, Cullen, George Fetch, Rothin; M'Rae, Rawgowan; Shepherd, Craibstone, Fortune, Portsoy, George Milne, Dytach, John Winchester, Loanhead; Leys, Cullen; Clark, Birkenbog, J. Hay, Brackenhills, Smith, Upper Blairock; Benzie, Blackhillock; Duncan, Langlanburn; Simpson, Woodside, &c.

Among estate officials and employes present were—Messrs M'Kenzie, Sharpe, Fowlie, J. Moir, Hardy, Beaton, Morton, W. Davidson, L. Beaton, Farquhar, Dryden, M'Rae, Cameron, Nicholson, J. Nicholson, Dustan, Desson,

Esslemont, M'Gregor, Eddie, J. Bowie, W.
Bowie, J Smith, Geddes, A. Taylor, Burnett,
J. Allan, C Allan, G. Mitchell, J Stuart, J
Clark, J Clark, jun, Watson, Watson, jun.,
Lovey, Bremner, Barclay, Imlach, Munroe,
Strachan, Innes, Gray, Davidson, Barclay,
Ross, Middleton, Hunter, Watson, Stevens, A.
M'Rae, Hay, Riach, Seivwright, Hardy, jun,
M'Hattie, Kirk, Ingles, Dalgarno, Gray, Cibb,
Hunter Murdoch, Knowles, D Linton, Balfour,
Mowat, Smith, A. Fyle, Stephens, Fordyce,
Simpson, T. Paterson, R. Patterson, and W.
Milne

The procession, it should be said, was admirably marshalled by Mr Hope, chief constable, with the assistance of Deputy Chief Constable Slorach and many other officers, and under their guidance all the arrangements operated very smoothly.

At Castle Grant.

A run of under two hours brought the special train to the private station at Castle Grant Here, another hearse, with mourning carriages, was in waiting and on the roadway, at the entrance to the policies, were clusters of people who displayed their sympathy with the ceremony that they saw Amongst those who joined the procession at the private station were Mr Grant Smith, factor, Mr Brown, wood manager; Mr Eric Anderson, Mr Gilbert, estate office; Mr Hastilow, Palace Hotel, Dr Barclay, Grantown, Mr Robert Grant, Muckerach; Mr W Macdonald Home Farm; Mr John Cumming, Mr A. Cumming, and Mr W Cumming, keepers, Mr James Shand, keeper, and Mr John Stuart The coffin was transferred, and a procession having been formed, the last stage of the journey to Castle Grant was accomplished. The coffin was carried through the main hall of the ancient granite castle of the Grants, and placed on trestles at the foot of the staircase. Here, indeed, the Chieftainess of a great and historic clan was at home, for ranged round the walls of the hall are the pikes of the Strathspey Fencibles, and a great assortment of weapons of Highland warfare, while aloft are suspended the Fencibles' ancient frayed banners. During the afternoon and evening an opportunity was given to the people of Grantown and neighbourhood to show their respect to the departed, and early in the afternoon a large body of children, accompanied by their teachers, marched in procession from Grantown to Castle Grant and reverently filed passed the coffin; whilst later large numbers of older people paid their last tribute of respect to the memory of one who had so graciously and considerately discharged the duties of lady of the manor. And thus the evening came peacefully down in the valley of the Spey, whither had come for her last rest a lady held in these Highland glens and straths in the utmost veneration.

Thursday morning dawned dull and hazy in the forest and heath-clad country of the Grants. Clouds filled the valleys, over them there appeared on occasion the lofty peak of some distant hill, the sides of which were enshrouded in mist. From time to time the sun's rays dispelled the autumn gloom, but the periods of sunshine were brief and the series of ceremonies of the day were gone through under conditions that seemed to be a fitting accompaniment to solemnities so great. At Castle Grant the Highland character of the obesquies was the paramount feature of the day's experiences. Here Lady Seafield ruled as Chieftainess over a great Highland territory; here she was at home in the ancient Highland seat of the family, all around is a wide district of romance and story that are intimately associated with the clan and its successive heads, and here she had been tenderly borne to be put to rest amid the loving tributes of her clansmen in the heart of a typical Highland country. Thousands of people were present on

Thursday at Castle Grant, other thousands lined the main street of Grantown as the stately procession passed along, between the town and the mausoleum at Duthil, the last resting-place of all, many people were to be seen by the roadside, and by hamlets, looking at the scene that was passing before their eyes, and at Duthil there had met a large company of ladies and gentlemen, of young men and maidens, and little children, to witness the lady whom they revered passing into the silence of the tomb. Many of the distinguished mourners who were present wore Highland dress, and the essential character of the ceremonies was further emphasised by the plaintive notes of the bagpipes as they came swelling over the woods and awakened responsive echoes in many hearts. All classes were represented Here were Highland gentlemen whose family names are entwined in our rugged island story; here were landed proprietors, the owners of fair and broad acres, from all over the north, here were substantial farmers, men of business from the towns, of professional men very many, and here also were crofters and cottagers, drawn from many a lone hillside—all classes there were, all met for a common sad purpose, and all mourning the death of a lady who in her every grace nobly adorned the great and responsible position she was called upon to fill

The severe grey structure of the ancient castle, plain it is in architectural design, but the very embodiment of strength, was the meeting place of all the many mourners who found their way on Thursday to Grantown-on-Spey A great many came in motors—never perhaps has this part of Speyside seen so many beautifully appointed cars; the morning trains were all heavily laden, from Tomintoul and many other outlying districts horsed conveyances brought hundreds of people, and a long special train that was run from Inverness and Forres brought a huge contingent of people from the lower parts of the country. As they entered the policies to each one was handed a sprig of green and fragrant spruce, the floral badge of the Grants, and practically every one wore it as a buttonhole during the day, and probably many have kept it as a memento of the last scene that will be associated with one whom they held in such respectful admiration. Then there was a short walk through the charming policies, abounding in a wealth of beauty and grace as they do at present under the influences of the advancing year. Those magnificent firs and limes, the spreading beeches, the massive oaks present a gorgeous scene in their golden tints of early autumn In a field near the castle a number of handsome Highland cattle, some of them with magnificent heads, were gently browsing, and recalled the pride that Lady Seafield ever took in the many showyard successes won by members of her famous fold. In the park before the house many deer were to be seen nibbling at the grass that in parts is still sweet and tender, some of them so tame that they came to the side of the fence to be fondled by children. Before noon had come, a great gathering had met at the castle. As they arrived they passed in single file under the plain arched doorway through the hall and by the side of the coffin at the foot of the staircase where all that was mortal of Lady Seafield lay amid the warlike relics of the past, under the drooping and ancient banners of the Strathspey Fencibles, and below the gaze of an early chieftain whose portrait shows a powerful figure standing with targe and curved sword held aloft. On the coffin, in addition to the pall of tartan, were two wreaths. The one at the head in white and pink carnations was from Captain Baird, and it bore the words—"With loving devotion and unbounded admiration,—David." The other was in white heather, from the Earl and Countess of Cassillis. The bier, resting here amid these storied banners, with at hand ancient pikes and firelocks and other warlike accoutrements seemed somehow to fill one's ideal of the going hence of the loved Chieftainess of a great Highland clan

Shortly after noon the coffin was carried from its resting place in the castle by a number of estate employes and placed on a raised dais in front of the building Around it gathered the great concourse of mourners who, with uncovered head, and with reverential heart and mien took part in the religious service that followed. It was very impressive, and through the silence of the still autumn air, in a scene the peaceful tranquility of which seemed to give the needful setting of repose, the voices of the officiating clergymen rose clear and distinct The immediate surroundings were full of colour There was the coffin with its precious burden and its tribute of flowers At its head stood the clergymen in official dress. Round the coffin were grouped the chief mourners and the bearers of names distinguished in the country's annals Mingled among the chief mourners were a number of ladies, including the Countess Cassillis, Mrs Campbell, Old Cullen; Mrs Davidson, Cullen; Mrs Smith and Miss Grant. There were many in Highland dress, and all were in mourning. In the great throng that stood around in close order and that maintained an impressive silence were to be seen here and there the scarlet robes of the representatives of various municipalities, and above the heads of the mourners there were to be seen the draped halberds with which they were accompanied. Farther on little knots of people stood around among the trees, and for an effective setting there were the tints of the glowing woods and far away the heathery and rocky heights of some of the Cairngorms.

The service was conducted by Rev. D. Young, pastor of that Inverallan Memorial Church which was gifted to the parish and to the Church of Scotland by the late Countess in loving memory of a husband and son, and by Rev T. S Cargill, minister of the parish of Cromdale. It was begun by Mr Cargill leading in prayer as follows—

"Almighty God, our Heavenly Father, who art our refuge and strength and a very present help in time of trouble, enable us we pray Thee to put our trust in Thee, so to fear Thy holy Word, that through patience and the comfort of the Scriptures we may have hope and, seeing that we have a High Priest who is touched with the feeling of our infirmities, may we come boldly unto the Throne of Grace that we may obtain mercy and find grace. Help us in this time of need through Jesus Christ our Lord."

Mr Cargill read also selected portions of Scripture The first was from that eloquent Psalm which says—"For a thousand years in Thy sight are but as yesterday when it is past, and as a watch in the night Thou carriest them away as with a flood; they are as a sleep. In the morning they are like grass which groweth up, in the morning it flourisheth and groweth up; in the evening it is cut down and withereth." "We spend our years as a tale that is told " There were read also those portions of St John's Gospel and of the Revelation that were used at the service at Cullen House, and thereafter Mr Young led in the following prayer—

O God most mighty and most merciful who pitiest them that fear Thee like as a father pitieth his own children, who knoweth our frame and rememberest that we are dust, look upon us in Thy great compassion whom Thou hast brought into the presence of sorrow and under the dark shadow of death. In the silence of this hour speak to us of eternal things and, with our spirits sinking before the mystery of life and of death, comfort us with the assurance that neither life nor death can ever separate us from Thy love as it is in Christ Jesus our Lord. O Christ, Thou man of sorrows, whom Thyself didst weep beside the grave, Thou too hast trod the way of anguish and tasted the bitterness of death; by our guilt which Thou hast borne, by our suffering which Thou hast endured, and by Thine own manifold mercies we beseech Thee to hear us. Lord grant now Thy peace unto Thy servants, and forsake us not in the hour of death We yield Thee hearty thanks O God most High for all Thy saints who have been lights in the world in their several generations and who, having accomplished their warfare, have passed to their reward, and entered into their rest. We remember before Thee in thanksgiving and faith and hope and love those most dear unto ourselves who have fallen asleep in Jesus, and especially this day we remember her, Thine handmaid, whom Thou hast taken to Thyself. We thank Thee for her long and honoured and useful life that in the high place where Thou didst set her she ever gave example of meek and gentle spirit of industry, and dutifulness, of reverence and prayerfulness, of godliness and trust. We remember the strange and clouded way by which Thou didst lead her, the house left unto her desolate and heart pierced through with many sorrows, but we praise Thee O Thou God most faithful that in all the darkness of her life Thou didst not leave her nor forsake her. We bless Thee that sorrow taught her loving kindness, that trial led her closer to Thy feet, and that her night of weeping was brightened with promises of Christ. For her tender compassion with all in tribulation, for the heart that was quick to feel and the hands that were ready to help, for duties faithfully done, for burdens bravely borne, for sorrows patiently sanctified and a great trust nobly fulfilled we give Thee thanks. For the love so richly given to her, for the light and the peace of her long time, for the faith in which she lived and the hope in which she died, we give Thee thanks The Lord giveth and the Lord taketh away, blessed be the name of the Lord And we magnify Thy holy name, that her trials and temptations being ended, that all the pains and dangers of this mortal life, sickness and death being parted, her spirit is with Thee in joyful reunion with the dear ones gone before her in Thy home of peace, where there shall be no more death neither sorrow nor sighing, for the former things are passed away I heard a voice from Heaven saying unto me— "Write from henceforth blessed are the dead which die in the Lord, yea, saith the Spirit, for they rest from their labours" Oh, God, the Holy Ghost, Lord and giver of life, the only comforter of the afflicted, visit with Thy tender consolation these Thy servants that they sorrow not as those who have no hope, be pitiful unto them from whom Thou hast taken away one who was most dear In their darkness may Thy light shine, and in their sorrow may they be filled with Thy peace which passeth all understanding We commend them unto Thee Bless unto them and scantify every pure remembrance of her who hath fallen asleep, lifting up their thoughts that they may desire things above, and that, where their treasure is their hearts may be also, even with Thee, oh blessed Spirit, in whom do live eternally the spirits of the children's God. O God, hear us, support us all the day long of this troublous life until the shades lengthen and the evening comes and our pilgrimage is ended and our work is done. Then in Thy mercy grant us a safe haven and a holy rest and peace at the last, through Jesus Christ, our Lord.

Mr Young then recited the Lord's Prayer and pronounced the benediction and the impressive ceremony ended.

Then the procession was formed So admirable were the arrangements that for that, despite its length, and the vast number of people who took part in it, a few minutes sufficed. Before the last part had left Castle Grant, the first extended far along the avenue—was indeed out of sight for the most part concealed in the wealth of greenery that still adorns the woods. There marched first the police escort of the Morayshire force, under Mr Mair, chief constable Then came eleven pipers of the 2nd Seaforth Highlanders from Fort George, whose music added an affecting and appealing element to the solemnities of the day. The cortege that followed was arranged in the following order—

>County and burgh of Inverness.
>County and burgh of Elgin.
>Burgh of Grantown.
>County of Nairn
>Burgh of Forres.
>County and burgh of Banff.
>Burgh of Cullen.
>Burgh of Keith.
>Burgh of Portsoy
>Burgh of Rothes.
>Clan Grant Society.
>>General Public.
>Tenantry of Strathspey and inhabitants of Grantown.
>>Tenantry of Glen Urquhart
>>Tenantry of Elgin, Rothes, and Birnie.
>>Tenantry of Cullen, Boyne, and Keith.
>>Clergy of all denominations.
>>Estate employees.
>>HEARSE.
>>Lady Seafield's carriage (closed and unoccupied).
>>Cars with wreaths
>>Family carriages.
>>Mourning carriages (provided).
>>Waggonettes (provided).
>>Other horse conveyances.
>>Motors.

Some of the civic representatives wore their gorgeous robes of office, and the Provost of Banff wore his handsome chain of office, and these gave a touch of colour to the sombre scene. The hearse was, as at Cullen, drawn by four handsome black horses, and in Lady Sea-

field's carriage, a touching feature, unoccupied
and with blinds drawn, was another pair of
beautiful black horses driven by Mr Nicholson.
So numerous were the wreaths that for their
conveyance three cars were necessary—cars
draped with purple, and when occupied exhibited a most beautiful and wealthy display of
the most lovely floral tributes In that order
the long procession started It was well over
a mile long and was of a nature that was fitted
to impress deeply all who took part in it or
who witnessed its passing. The moment the
march was begun, there uprose from the pipes
the wailing strains of "The Flowers of the
Forest." The music had a wonderful effect as
it sounded and resounded through the trees
and thickets and penetrated away beyond the
policies And then soon the pipers changed to
"The Land o' the Leal," and as the tender and
affecting music that is associated with Lady
Nairne's best known poetical work filled the
air, there were some who found it hard to
check an outburst of the natural emotions it
evoked, emphasised as it was by the striking
scene that was all around That was the tune
that was played when Grantown was reached
High Street here, right almost from the castle
gates to the other extremity of the town, was
thickly lined on both sides with vast crowds of
men and women and young people who regarded the passing of the cortege with a mournful
interest that was very evident. Not a few
women were to be seen sobbing heavily. The
impressive silence that reigned in the town
was broken only by the laments of the pipes
or the solemn tolling of the bell. All business
was suspended, and with the heads of all uncovered, and with everywhere looks of reverence, the great company passed on. Numerous
photographers did what they could to obtain
a favourable view of such a scene as is not
often witnessed. Slowly and with measured

E

pace the procession passed through the long main street of the burgh, past the Ian Charles Hospital which the Countess founded in memory of her son, past the Christian Institute, in whose interest her ladyship did so much, past scenes that were among the most familiar and the best loved of her life, until at last the end of the town was reached, where, at the junction of the road below the Highland Railway station, all those on foot divided and allowed the carriages to pass through on the final stage of their journey to Duthil. And thus Castle Grant had been left, and the outskirts of the capital of the Grant country had been reached. The Chieftainess had been so far accompanied by thousands of her clansmen and friends. The number who went on the last journey was necessarily fewer, so that it may be well here to note some representative men who were present—a list very far from full but that may serve to illustrate the character of the great company that had met on Speyside on this mission of sadness and sorrow.

The chief mourners were Captain David Baird, M V O, younger of Newbyth, grand-nephew; the Earl of Cassillis, grand-nephew, the Earl of Seafield; Mr William G C. Gladstone of Hawarden, M P., grand-nephew; Mr William Arthur Baird of Lennoxlove, grand-nephew; The Mackintosh of Mackintosh, Sir Reginald Macleod of Macleod, K C.B, and Mr James Campbell, LL D., Old Cullen, Cullen (pall-bearers), and the Rev. Lord Blythswood, Mr Stewart, younger of Southwick, Mr Garden Alexander Duff of Hatton, and Mr Evan J. Cuthbertson, W S, Edinburgh. Among the other mourners present were the Duke of Richmond and Gordon, K G , Sir John Macpherson Grant, Bart., of Ballindalloch; Mr Bradley Martin, Balmacaan ; Lord Cheylesmore, K.C.V.O ; Mr Grant of Elchies; Mr Gordon Duff of Drummuir; Mr Alistair Grant of Drumduan; Colonel Forbes of Rothiemay; Captain Forbes, Rothiemay Castle; Mr Grant of Glenmorriston; Colonel Johnston of Lesmurdie; Mr Baillie of Dochfour; Mr Grant of Rothiemurchus; Mr Wm. Whitelaw, chairman of the H.R. Company; Sir George Abercromby, Bart., of Forglen; Mr R D. Holt, M P , Forest Lodge, Mr Arthur Sassoon, Tulchan Lodge; General Sir H. Grant, Colonel Hugo Grant, Professor Harrower of Aberdeen University; Mr Lewis Grant and Mr James Grant, representing the Glasgow Clan Grant Society; Mr James Mackay, president of the Mod; Mr Grant Smith, factor, Grantown; Mr Samson, factor, Elgin; Colonel Vivian, Delfur; Sir Spencer M. Wilson, Mr Hugh Northcote, London; Mr Davidson, York House, Cullen; Mr Grant, Ruallan; Mr H. Ogilvie Grant, London; Mr Park, general manager, Highland Railway, Dr Alexander Ross, Inverness; Mr William Mackay, Inverness; Mr Jamieson, county clerk, Inverness; Mr G R. Mackessack of Ardgye, convener of the county of Elgin; Mr Grant of Kincorth, Forres; Mr Duncan Shaw, Inverness, ex-Provost Gossip Inverness; Mr A Macdonald, sheriff clerk of Inverness-shire, &c.

As is noted above many municipal and other local governing bodies were represented. The Town Council of Grantown had naturally a full representation, headed by the Provost of the burgh, Dr Barclay. From Elgin also there came municipal representatives, with Provost Wilson at their head. Inverness Town Council was also officially represented, Provost Birnie leading the deputation from the Highland capital. Provost Douglas and other members of the Council came from Forres, along with the town clerk, Colonel Urquhart, M.V.O. There was a full representation of Cullen Town Council—Provost Gregor, Bailies Forbes and Urquhart, Dean of Guild Macleod, Treasurer Simpson, and Councillors Ingram, Leys, Masson, Harthill, Turner, and Stewart, with Mr Paterson, town clerk, and Mr John Simpson, in uniform, carrying a draped halberd. From Banff Town Council there were present Provost Christie, Bailie Cumming, and Councillor F. A. Watt, with Mr James Grant, town and county clerk, and Mr P Hutcheon, in Highland dress, carrying a halberd, draped From Keith Town Council there attended Provost Cameron and Bailies Stewart and M'Connachie, wearing their ornate official robes, with Mr J. G. Fleming, town clerk There was a large representation also from Portsoy Town Council, including Bailies Gray and Macdonald, Dean of Guild Rae, and Councillor James Kemp, with Mr James Young, town clerk The Town Council of Rothes was also represented, with Provost Ross at their head.

Among the many others present were—

Dr Fergusson, Banff; Mr Hope, chief constable of Banffshire, Major Chinn, Portsoy; Mr George Smith, Ordens, Rev. J. G Ledingham, Boyndie; Rev. G. M. Park, Deskford, Messrs Forbes Rettie; Smith, Thriepland, Macpherson, Auchmillie, Garden, Brankanentham; Lewis Beaton, Cullen House Home Farm, J D Sharpe, Cullen House estates office; James Moir, Wm. Beaton, and Wm. Davidson, do; Alex. Gordon, bank agent, Cullen; James Gordon, Inspector of Poor, Cullen, John Brown, Cullen; Kitchen, Clune; A. Maclean, Cullen; Alex. Macdonald, implement maker, Portsoy; Miller, Grant Arms, Cullen, Faulds, dentist, Cullen; Mackenzie, forester; Morton, gardener; Burnett, Tochineal tile works; Cameron, head gamekeeper; John Eadie, Seatown Cottage, Cullen; J. R. Moir Cullen, Rev. J. M'Intyre, and Messrs Donaldson, Sutherland, Addison, Bruce, and Wood, of Portknockie; Dr M'Hardy, Cullen; A. T. Rettie, Cullen; Green, Whyntie; Blacklaws, ground officer; John A. Colville, solicitor, Portsoy; Wm. Forbes, Cowhythe; Maclennan, Bogton; Gunn, Kilnhillock, Thomson, Kindrought; D. O. Stevenson, Durn; Rev. J. C. MacGregor, Fordyce; James Grant, Glenconglass, Kirkmichael; W. Sim, Tomintoul; G.

G M'Robie, Portsoy; Hogg, road surveyor, Elgin; John Macpherson, Mains of Mulben; Hugh Stewart, Elgin, A Murray, Schoolhouse, Birnie; Rev. J. Kennedy, Birnie; J. S George, Inspector of Poor, Hopeman; Alex. Grant, Crooksmill; Wm. Stewart, Birkenburn; Robert Allan, Bush; A. Annand, bank agent, Keith; James Annand, ironmonger, Keith; George Petrie Hay, Keith; George Cameron, South Bogbain; Alex. Brown, Drakemyres; Wm. M'Connachie, Aultash; J Fraser, Auchroisk; G Fraser, Belnabreich; James M'William, Stoneytown; Chas Macgregor, retired schoolmaster, Keith; Geo A Stephen, Keith; John W. Kynoch, Isla Bank, P. Kynoch Shand, Keith; James Auchinachie, Mid Street, Keith; H Taylor, Strathmill; James Milne, Shalloch; Mr George Davidson and Mr James Ward, of Seafield estates office, Keith, John Fowlie, architect, Cullen House, Wm. Guthrie, Brunton; A. Bell, ground officer, Rothes, W. M'Bain, ground officer, Glenurquhart, Rev Mr M'Farlane, Kingussie, Rev. Mr Robertson, Nethy Bridge; John Grant, bank agent, Grantown, George Harvey, Rosehall, do , Stephen, forester, Nethy Bridge, John Grant, Muckerach, G. M'Innes, Tormore, Advie; James Allan, Ballintomb; J and C Robertson, Tullochgribban, A. Gordon, Finlarig; Major Cumming, Curr; Dr Hutcheson, Grantown; W Forsyth, town clerk, Grantown, H. Macpherson, Duier, Advie; J. M'Ainsh, Congash; J. Grant, Garvault; D. G. Grant, Dalvey; Maclennan, rector, Grantown; H. M. S. Mackay, Elgin; John Thomson, bookseller, Grantown; Roberts, chief engineer, Highland Railway; Burgess, Mains of Cromdale; Rev. John Liddell, Advie; Rev. Mr Jenkins, Rothes; Robb, chairman of Rothes Parish Council; Mackintosh, National Bank, Grantown; J. T. Garrioch, factor, Beauly; Marshall, Dundurcas; Lawson, Dandaleith; Grant, Drumbain, Rev. Hamilton Dunnett, Inveraven; R Mackinnon, forester, Duthil; Rev. Gavin Lang, Inverness, Rev Mr Maclean, Abernethy; Rev Mr Maclean, Cullen; Rev. Mr Macpherson, Bourtie; Angus Urquhart, Inverness; R. Dick Stuart, Rothes; Rev. S. Ree, Boharm; Alex. Garden, Windyhills, Grange, &c.

At Duthil.

At the extremity of the burgh of Grantown there was begun the final stage of the long journey. As has been said, the great company of mourners opened up at the junction of the road to the Highland Railway station and allowed the funeral car, the three cars with the wreaths, Lady Seafield's carriage, and the mourning coaches to pass through on their way to Duthil seven miles distant. For those other mourners who had hitherto been on foot and who anxiously desired to accompany the remains to the end additional conveyances were provided. Mr Hastilow, Palace Hotel, who was entrusted with the horse and carriage arrangements, was responsible for supplying over one hundred horses, the Seaforth pipers found accommodation in a powerful motor belonging to the railway company, and there were a large number of private motors, so that the wheeled procession extended along the roadway for a distance of a mile and a half, and in magnitude alone it presented a striking spectacle. The route to the churchyard traverses scenery of a typically Highland kind—moor and heather, expanses of forest, rocky hillsides, with in the distance the mighty Cairngorms, and at many points was heard the rush of streams at present at their lowest level. At many points on the route groups of people had gathered. Some were at a distance from the roadway, where no house seemed to be, and throughout, the houses that were passed, as had been the case at Grantown, had their blinds closely drawn, while everywhere the imposing procession of carriages and motors was witnessed with a silence and respectful sympathy that spoke eloquently of the harrowed feelings of many of the onlookers, many of whom were old men and women who could recall no doubt the day when the aged Countess had appeared among them first as a lovely bride, full of high hopes and with an inspiring outlook, and now carried before their eyes to the grave with her life's work nobly accomplished. At picturesque Dulnain Bridge there was quite a gathering of people, and at that point the mist lifted somewhat, and through beautiful Highland scenery the Cairngorms peered out, and one could more clearly see the purple heather on the fir-clad slopes, broken here and there by cultivated haugh and modest farm steading A feature near by was the still noble ruins of Muckerach Castle, a former stronghold of the Grants, whose bare gaunt walls still boldly look skyward. And soon, when an abrupt turn to the right was reached, the carriages were stopped, the mourners dismounted, and the last procession of all was formed In the deep shadow of the trees of a close fir plantation was the last resting place of the family. Here a considerable gathering of people had met. There were many women present and many little children. The pipers led the way up a bit of rising ground to the soul stirring strains of "Lochaber no More." At the entrance to the little churchyard, at the gate of which stood the aged parish minister, Rev Mr Bain, a pathetic figure, the Rev. Lord Blythswood stood waiting to receive the coffin, clad in his Anglican surplice and mourning stole. The procession moved slowly into the churchyard, and when the dirge of the pipes had died away, there was heard the voice of the noble clergyman reciting the solemn committal service—"I am the Resurrection and the Life." The pallbearers followed the coffin into the darkened interior, from which the voice of the officiating clergyman came to the throng outside. When the obsequies were over, once more there was heard over the calm and peaceful scene the tender, expressive music of the Highlanders. The piper of The Mackintosh of Mackintosh, Mr

Duncan Macdonald, at the bidding of his chief, played as few could so well that fine setting—"The Lament for the Only Son." It came as the climax and the end to a series of ceremonies that will have an abiding place in the memory of all who witnessed them. There are two mausoleums in the churchyard which have been the burying place of the family. In the one that was opened on Thursday was placed the body of the seventh Earl of Seafield, husband of the Countess, who died in 1881. Here also were brought the remains of their only son, Ian Charles, who died in 1884 The last vacant niche will be filled by the coffin of the late Countess. In the mausoleum on Thursday the coffins of husband and son were to be seen, lying side by side That of the Countess, now rejoining in the silence of the tomb those whose early deaths threw a shadow over the greater portion of her life, was placed temporarily at right angles to the others. The latter were still covered with wreaths, the Countess, up to a comparatively recent date having regularly visited the mausoleum The three coffins will now be placed together in a common recess, and the mausoleum will then be permanently closed After the chief mourners had left the mausoleum, after the office for the dead had been fully recited, when all had been done for the honoured dead that devoted mourners could do, an opportunity was given to the company of filing past the coffins and of seeing where three members of the great family are sleeping their last long sleep.

And thus there went down to the grave a lady, loved, admired, and revered, who has left her beneficent impress deep in the history of these north-eastern parts She passed away at a good old age after the work of her long life had been accomplished. She died full of years and rich in the love and regard of thousands, and she went to her grave amid such manifestations of sorrow and wholehearted sympathy and regret as are vouchsafed to few. Lady Seafield has become only a memory, but with her the mind will ever associate everything that is noble and womanly and the active virtues that belonged to a life that was guided by the highest of motives and that ever found its strength and its solace in time of deep sorrow as in periods of brightness in that Source which lies beyond this passing sphere.

The police arrangements were, in Morayshire, in the hands of Mr Mair, chief constable, while at Duthil, which is in Invernessshire, everything was admirably carried out under the supervision of Major Maclean, chief constable of that county. Messrs Beale and Pyper, Grantown, carried out the undertakers' arrangements from the arrival of the coffin at the private station at Castle Grant to the interment at Duthil.

A very large number of wreaths and floral tributes were received at Cullen House and Castle Grant. Those who sent these loving messages of regret and sorrow were—The Earl of Seafield, the Marquis and Marchioness of Ailsa, Culzean Castle, Ayr, the Earl and Countess of Cassillis, Sir David and Lady Baird and Miss Baird, Newbyth; Captain Baird; Mr William and Lady Hersey Baird, Erskine; Lord Charles and Lord Angus Kennedy, Lady Borthwick, 2, Upper Grosvenor Street London, W.; Mr J Grant Thomson and family, Mount Barker, Grantown, Mr H. H. S. Northcote, 18, Chapel Street, London, S W.; Miss Helen Fraser, 18, Glebe Avenue, Stirling, Miss Grant, 7, Sloane Street, London, S W.; Dr and Mrs Campbell, Old Cullen; Sir Mark and Lady M'Taggart Stewart; Mrs Gladstone, Hawarden Castle, Chester; Mrs Grant (late of Fordyce), Miss Grant and Miss C. S. Grant, Inglesby, Banchory; The office staff and heads of departments on the Cullen, Boyne, and Keith Districts of the Seafield Estates; the estate workmen in Cullen and Boyne Districts; Mr and Miss John A. Colville, Millburn, Portsoy; Mrs Graham Murray, Eva. and Ronnie, Glen Chess, Rickmansworth, Miss Stuart, Eaglescarnie, Haddingtonshire; the Town Council and other public bodies and officials of the Royal Burgh and Parish of Cullen, the estate officials on the Strathspey Estate, Colonel and Mrs Algernon Durand, 31, Park Lane, London, the Kirk Session of Inverallan; Sir John and Miss Innes, Edingight; Servants in Cullen House (two wreaths), Mr and Mrs Leybourne F. Davidson, York House, Cullen; Lady Cathcart, Cluny Castle, Miss Grant (of Grant), Tighnamara, Craigendoran, Helensburgh, the Earl and Countess of Aberdeen Vice Regal Lodge, Dublin, Mr and Mrs M'Leod Baxter, 7, Bute Mansions, Hillhead, Glasgow, Mr and Mrs Bradley Martin, Chesterfield Gardens, London; the Earl and Countess of Craven, 3, Chesterfield Gardens, London; Miss Kynoch, Strathlene; Mrs C. H. Murphay, J. L. Stephen, Abernethy, Dowager Lady Burton, Rangemore; Mr and Mrs Grant, Kincorth, Forres, Strathspey Farmer Club, Mr and Mrs J Grant Smith, Inverallan, Grantown; Mr and Mrs Sassoon, Tulchan; Mr Robert Grant, Muckerach Lodge, Grantown; Servants at Castle Grant, the employes of the Glenurquhart Estates; Mrs Smith, Miss Smith, and Miss Caroline Smith, Dulaig, Miss C. Thornewell, Rangemore; from Hazel Brae, Glenurquhart, Colonel and Mrs Payne Grant; Sir Reginald and Miss MacLeod; The Hon. Mrs Thomas Bruce and Miss Bruce; Mrs Duncan Baillie, Lochloy, Mrs N Hamilton Ogilvy; Dulnan Bridge School pupils, staff and friends; parishioners in Duthil; tenants in Cromdale and Advie; Miss Rae, The Hospital Grantown; Miss F. G. Grant, 7, Sloane Street, London, S.W.; Dr and Mrs Barclay, Grantown; Lord Rosebery; David T. Samson, Elgin, Sir John and Lady Macpherson Grant, Ballindalloch, patients and nurses in Ian Charles Cottage Hospital, Grantown; Evan J. Cuthbertson, W S, Edinburgh; Mr and Lady Mary Grant, Rothiemurchus; Sir Reginald and Lady Agnes MacLeod; Anne, Countess of Moray, Tarbert House, Kildary; Lord and Lady Lovat.

PULPIT AND OTHER REFERENCES.

In many northern pulpits reference was made on the Sunday succeeding her death to her beautiful life and character.

CULLEN PARISH CHURCH.

In the Cullen Parish Church, a church in which the late Countess of Seafield so frequently worshipped and towards which she showed such affectionate regard, there was a very large congregation. The pulpit and the Seafield pew and the galleries were draped in heavy black drapings. Just before the commencement of the service the Earl and Countess of Cassillis, Captain David Baird, M.V.O., Mr William Baird, grand-nephews of the late Countess, and Mr Cuthbertson, W S, Edinburgh, entered the church and took their seats in the family pew. The service opened with the playing as a voluntary of "O Rest in the Lord," a favourite piece of the late Countess. There followed the singing of Hymn 102, "When our Heads are Bowed with Woe." The Old Testament lesson was taken from Psalm xc., and its beautiful language, "We spend our years as a tale that is told," was very impressively read by Mr Maclean. Four verses of the same Psalm were afterwards sung by the congregation. The New Testament lesson was taken from I. Corinthians xv., and the plaintive "Peace, Perfect Peace" was then sung. After the sermon the congregation sang "Now the Labourer's Task is o'er" and "Sleep on Beloved." At the conclusion of the service the "Dead March" in "Saul" was played by Mr MacLeod, organist, and during its rendering the congregation remained standing.

Rev. W. G. G. Maclean preached from the text "Man goeth to his long home," and at the close he made feeling reference to the sad circumstances under which they were met that day. He spoke of the bereavements the late Countess had had to pass through, of the worthy manner in which she had carried out the traditional policy of the House of Grant in her regard for the welfare of her tenantry, of the universal esteem in which she was held, and of her attachment to the Church of Scotland. Continuing, Mr Maclean said:—There has been nothing more beautiful in the life of her whose loss we mourn to-day than the delight she found in the simple worship of this old church, hallowed to her by so many sweet memories. So long as health permitted, she worshipped with us here morning and evening, and there was no more devout worshipper than she, and on Communion Sundays, sitting at the Holy table with the poorest members of the community, she found real comfort and refreshment in the sacred feast. It was touching to see her with feeble step two years ago conduct our late King into this church and point out to the great monarch with obvious pride the different objects of interest. To you I need not speak of her kindness to the poor and the children, and her sympathy with the suffering and the sorrowing. One had only to see her enter, as she so often did, some humble dwelling and hear her words of encouragement and comfort to those in pain or sorrow to be convinced of the depth of her religious convictions. Truly she found her chief joy in doing good, and we cannot yet realise how irreparable is our loss, for the privileges we enjoyed were many and great. Long will we with gratitude remember all she did for the temporal comfort and moral and spiritual welfare of this community. Long will the name of Lady Seafield be held in grateful remembrance and her wise words and generous deeds will in years to come bring forth in many places the fruits of righteousness and peace. So far from fearing the approach of the last enemy, she longed for his coming, regarding death as a messenger of mercy to open the gateway to a fuller and more perfect life. And now, after more than four score years, a life of singular beauty and wonderful charm has come to a close like a stately vessel crossing the harbour bar after a long and weary voyage. She expressed a desire to go to sleep and, closing her eyes, she peacefully passed away from the trials and weariness of this life to the rest and reward of those who have borne with patience the heavy cross and done what they could in the service of their Lord. To those who feel most deeply the loss of her, whose life on earth has closed, it must be a comforting assurance that she has gone to where the earnest and the true find again those whom they have "loved long since and lost a while"—to the great beatific vision which is the reward of the faith, the love and the service of earth.

CULLEN U F CHURCH.

Part of the interior of the Cullen U.F. Church was also draped in black, and the service was of a nature appropriate to the sad occasion Rev G. Lithgow Wilson preached from "To them who by patient continuance in well-doing seek for glory and honour and immortality and eternal life." He spoke of the excellent Christian graces exhibited in the character of the late Countess of Seafield, of her fortitude in bereavement—"Her sincerity, her simplicity, her loftiness of soul won for her such profound respect as never could have been earned by a mere title and empty patronising airs Her tenantry loved her, her friends honoured her, her sovereign paid her the tribute of worthy acquaintance. As the minister of a congregation in which we have not a few aged folk, and several who sit out the long, long years in loneliness, I had the pleasure of hearing from time to time of the kindly, homely, Christian ministrations of the lady whose death we this day mourn. Experience had taught her the preciousness of sympathy, and many an errand did she make so that with her presence and testimony to the goodness of God she might give soothing and cheer to those in trouble. Even in her latest years she continued to carry out these missions of mercy when she might have found in her growing infirmities enough to occupy her thoughts Her heart went out to the poor and needy, and to her tenants, to her servants, to her King and country And she never forgot God To her the Saviour was precious. Most beautiful, then, in its pathos and fitting in its form has been the end of such a life As a child passes from its prattle and its play, so she has passed in sleep from the toil and moil and loneliness, passed home to be with Jesus Having lived those years at the door of her historic house, we cannot but grieve over the great loss which our burgh and parish have sustained by her ladyship's death We had come to regard ourselves almost as members of her household, and we venerated with no common sincerity her who ruled it. What shall our tribute to her memory be?—Not a mere monument in a cemetery, where her dust shall sleep with kindred dust until "the ancient graves be stirred." Not that, for there is a worthier Shall we not vow to take her Lord to be our Lord and serve Him as she did with such singular purity and grace?"

DESKFORD PARISH CHURCH.

Preaching in Deskford Parish Church from the words "Father unto Thy hands I commend my spirit," Rev G. M. Park said.—Few have lived so laborious a life, and few have been so touched by the finger of God Bereft of her husband and of her only child, she has presided with grace and dignity over the interests of the great House of Seafield for the last 27 years. How well she has discharged the onerous duties that fell to her lot as the owner of broad acres, the public prints will tell you. No doubt she was greatly dowered by Nature, and had a deep sense of responsibility as the representative of a great Highland chief; but her capacities were greatly enlarged by her own carefulness and sense of duty. Though she might well have left the supervision of her great estates to others, she yet chose to do it herself, and was most conscientiously strict in all business relations with her tenants And this constant attention to duty, coupled with a memory that forgot nothing, together with a remarkable insight and sympathy, made her one of the best known and most honoured of our great landed proprietors But it was the womanliness, the homeliness of her character that won for her the place she held in the affections of her tenants Gifted with a large and generous nature, she at once interested herself in all that concerned the welfare of her people; and her unfailing sympathy and tact, her kindness and generous help to every form of distress soon established a bond of affection between herself and them. In all her family relationships she was a pattern of propriety and virtue, and when sorrows began to crowd upon her the hearts of her people went out to her in ever-increasing sympathy.

DESKFORD U F CHURCH

Rev James Morrison, Deskford U F Church, preached from the words "For our citizenship is in Heaven, from whence also we look for the Saviour, the Lord Jesus Christ," and said —Of Lady Seafield there can be but one opinion She was a sincere and most amiable Christian lady, whose life bore ample testimony to the reality and strength of her faith. Although she had great worldly possessions and enjoyed high rank, she lived the life of a humble Christian and ever remembered that her citizenship was in Heaven, from whence also she looked for her Saviour, the Lord Jesus Christ. As a landlady owning and presiding over vast estates, Lady Seafield gained the gratitude and affection of her tenants by her liberality and kindness, being ever ready to help the struggling as well as to encourage the pushing and the successful Taught sympathy by her own bitter experience, she was specially thoughtful for the widow, and many such have had abundant reason to bless her name. The poor and the sick always found in her a willing friend and helper, and she was ever ready to assist every good cause She took a special interest in everything connected with the welfare of young and old in our own parish of Deskford; and we, ourselves, as a congregation, benefited by her liberality when we renovated our church, and on other occasions. Her ladyship's memory will be long cherished among us for her high Christian character, her liberality to her tenants, and her many good works.

SEAFIELD PARISH CHURCH.

Rev. James M'Intyre, in the course of a touching reference to the late Countess of Seafield, said.—I may refer to those of her benefactions in which we as a community and congregation have shared and been benefited by. One of the piers in our harbour bears her honoured name, and very properly, considering the liberality with which she contributed to the building of the harbour, and the part she took in connection with its opening, while it seems but yesterday since she was so kind as furnish us with a recreation park. Following out and giving effect to the wishes of her son, who, alas! ran his race so quickly, she was mainly instrumental in endowing our church and raising the district to the status of an ecclesiastical parish, while later on she also gave us what very few quoad sacra parishes have—a glebe. Her interest in the poor was manifested in many ways, and in none perhaps more wisely and more to their profit than in the clothing clubs which she instituted in the different parishes of her estates. Having herself known what it is to mourn like the widow of Nain, her sympathy went forth in full measure to the widow, especially to those among us, of whom, alas! the number is not small, who had lost husband or son by the devouring sea. Her life was rich beyond that of many of her own rank, or indeed of any rank, in good deeds, the outcome of a thoughtful and kindly heart. Hers was a deeply religious nature, and it was in religion she sought and found the consolation and support her sorrows needed. Her faith was strong and well-founded—she knew in whom she had believed—and she had lived under a constant sense of the unseen and the eternal. To her, while active and energetic in the duties of the day, the other, the spiritual world, was as real as, or more real than, this. She longed, though in no morbid way, for the fuller revelation death would bring her and the restoration of the loved ones whom the Heavenly Father had taken so many years before to His nearer presence And now, though long delayed, she has had her wish granted, and she has reached her abiding home at last.

FORDYCE U.F. CHURCH.

In the Fordyce U F Church, Rev James Robertson said in the course of his reference that having to drink deeply at the wells of sorrow herself, the late Countess of Seafield was ever ready to extend sincere sympathy to others similarly situated. If the cloud of sorrow hung over any home within her domain, she did her best to dispel it and to bring joy to the troubled heart. In many a home in the neighbourhood of Cullen House and Castle Grant her ministries of love will be long remembered The secret of her sympathy and love lay in the fact that she had learned the sympathy and love of Christ, and thus in some measure was able to show to others what she had learned to be His will and spirit. She set before herself a high ideal of Christian service, and to reach it was her constant endeavour. Her Christian faith and devotion were revealed in acts of kindness, and she dignified her position by a spirit of gracious humility She felt that her position was a responsible one, and so used it with judgment and discretion To the poor on her large estates her passing away will constitute the removal of a true and loving friend The congregation then sang " Now the labourer's task is o'er."

PORTSOY EAST U F. CHURCH.

Rev. Mr Simmers prepared a reference, which was read by Rev. A. B. Rogerson, Banff, who was officiating for him on Sunday:—Few landlords have left a more grateful memory than Lady Seafield has done. In circumstances which, owing to the uncertainties of succession, might have induced many a one to neglect the estate, and to further only their own interests, or the interest of personal friends, she stood true to those of the estate, and to the welfare of the tenant both present and to come. Being

of a strong nature, she sometimes came into
collision with sections of the community, as
all strong and confident natures will do, but
she ever aimed at what she believed to be
right and spared no pains to achieve it. She
had at all times a deep sympathy with true
religion, and with evangelical doctrine. She
was also much interested in the cause of temperance. As proof of her interest in both we, in Portsoy, found her a generous helper when she gave £50 towards the securing of our Y.M.C A. Institute, whose object was and is the promotion of evangelistic and temperance work.

PORTSOY PARISH CHURCH

Rev. A. M. Gibson, in Portsoy Parish Church said :—All along her ladyship had proved herself to be a model proprietrix, living for the most part of the year in her beautiful northern home, taking a warm and intelligent interest in all that concerned the welfare of her numerous tenantry, rejoicing with them in their prosperity, and in seasons of agricultural depression not only sympathising with them, but helping them in a tangible way with the thoughtful and welcome abatement of rent, ever acting on the principle of "Live and let live," and that property had its duties as well as its rights Her knowledge of her tenants was wonderful. The name of the smallest crofter was as familiar to her as the name of the largest farmer on the estates. All were equal in her eyes. In seasons of sickness and bereavement, who was more sympathetic or more attentive than the late lamented Dowager Countess? She herself drank deeply of sorrow's cup, and she knew what to say and how to say it in the hour of family affliction Her benevolence, her practical help to clothing societies, her varied and discriminating charities are widely known and appreciated, though on her part they were done so quietly and unostentatiously as if she did not wish her left hand to know what her right hand did

ST JOHN'S, PORTSOY.

Rev. John Southby said Lady Seafield was

called to fulfil a high calling, and was for ever at the call of those in want, sickness, and sorrow of every kind. I have only had the privilege of knowing her a short time, having so lately come to Portsoy, but I found her a great friend to St John's, always ready to do what she could. Only to-day there are tokens of her love; the lovely flowers on the altar are her gifts. She has been in past years a worshipper in this Church, and also till this present time a seatholder I feel that I cannot say all, as so many can who have known her a lifetime, but one can see in a short time how she walked "worthy of her calling."

BANFF PARISH CHURCH.

At the close of his sermon on Sunday forenoon in Banff Parish Church, Dr Bruce said that in the late Dowager Countess of Seafield, whose death they all sincerely mourned, every good cause had for long found a friend, every one in sorrow a sister, every one in need a benefactor. Her ideal was to be all that her position required of a large landowner entrusted with great responsibilities and holding in her hand the prosperity and wellbeing of a numerous tenantry. He was certain that no deserving enterprise for the good of the community ever appealed to her sympathetic soul in vain; and her generosity was so manifold and varied that few people knew its expansive range. He was bound in gratitude to speak of her uniform kindness as a heritor in the parish and a helpful friend to their Sunday Schools. He knew her first of all as the wife of the 7th Earl of Seafield, who was patron of the parish of Banff and presented him to the living on the recommendation of the people. Of his and her kindness then he had a very grateful recollection — all the more that it had continued throughout his ministry. Her lofty example of living had been a constant help to them all; and he knew it was the outcome of a sincere piety and a humble faith. Religion had been the abiding strength of her life, and had helped her, amid a succession of the most painful trials a wife and a mother could be called to go through, to maintain that beautiful tranquil balance that impressed all who met her.

It gave constancy to her every purpose and consistency to all her actions In the storm and stress of life it filled her heart with love and her soul with peace, and by its sanctions and motives she was enabled to choose her own independent line of duty. Few women have filled a more useful place in society or had more promptly bought up every opportunity of doing good To her, all obligation took the form of a joyous service. Her genuine piety gave all her work as landlady, as patron, or as humble church member, the fine qualities of stability and permanence, qualities which came to be woven into the whole texture of her character. That was the reason why people everywhere admired, loved, and looked up to Caroline, Countess-Dowager of Seafield.

BOYNDIE PARISH CHURCH.

Sunday was the occasion of the thanksgiving service for the good harvest in Boyndie Parish Church.

At the close of the sermon Rev. J. G Ledingham made the following reference to the death of Lady Seafield —"As we gathered together to-day to thank God for the overflowing cup— our barns filled with plenty, the presses bursting out with new wine—which this year He has given us, our thoughts ever and again wandered away to that silent death chamber, where lie the mortal remains of her at whose hands we hold these fertile fields. It was with deep regret we heard the end had come, and it is fitting that here we should make some reference to one who for so long had been deeply interested in us and in our welfare. Personally she was unknown to most of us, still we feel that in Lady Seafield we had a kind and sympathetic friend, who while just, was also generous. In this district, where are situated her most fertile possessions, she was particularly interested, the comfortable homesteads and substantial steadings all testifying to the care she had for the welfare of her people, the many improvements bearing witness to the zeal with which she had administered her wide estates. Of the Church she was a loyal supporter, following in this respect, as in all others, the example of her late husband and son For long her life must have been a lonely one—it is now many years since her house was left unto her desolate. For her the stages of life's journey must have been measured by those taken from her rather than by those that are left Still, her life was green to the end, for she found her joy in the joy of others, in the welfare of her people, in the wise administration of the great trust committed to her." At the conclusion of the sermon, as a token of respect to her memory, the congregation stood while the "Dead March" was played.

FINDOCHTY U F CHURCH.

Rev J. W. M'Kee, preaching on the text "Honourable women not a few," made feeling reference to the death of Lady Seafield.

KEITH PARISH CHURCH.

In the Parish Church of Keith on Sunday forenoon Rev. Sydney Smith at the conclusion of the sermon said—"I feel I am but complying with the unspoken desire of many in making a reference, however brief, to the lady who has through these many years so nobly fulfilled the trust committed to her. No portrait could do justice to her that did not attempt to convey her devout spirit, her queenlike dignity and grace, her remarkable gifts of administration, her decision of character, the inward resource whereby she sustained crushing sorrows, and faced again and yet again with high heart the responsibilities of her exalted station Nor must we forget that liberality whereby she devised liberal things Her generosity to the town and this congregation has often moved us to sincere gratitude. We owe it to her that we have a beautiful park and a justly admired avenue. It was she who inaugurated and has regularly supported one of our most useful local philanthropies, I mean the Seafield Clothing Club As a church and congregation we recall her interest in our Sunday scholars, and her kindly wish expressed in an annual gift that they should not miss as summer returned their day by the sea, or among the woods and flowers of the field,

The deed whereby she made over to the Kirk Session of this church, for all time coming, the ground which preserves to view the stately proportions of the edifice is evidence in the same direction."

NORTH U F CHURCH, KEITH.

In the North U.F Church Rev. H. Fitzpatrick, at the close of his forenoon sermon, said—"In this district and beyond many mourn to-day the death of one who was greatly esteemed, respected, and loved, namely, the amiable proprietrix, Lady Seafield She was ever kind and good to the poor and needy, and ever ready practically to help the deserving strugglers amid adverse circumstances on her large estates This beneficent lady will be greatly missed by many. She was ever kind and considerate to her tenants, whom she delighted to see happy and contented. She was one who abounded in every good and philanthropic work that had for its object the good and prosperity of her people. She will long live in the affection and grateful remembrance of her people Spared to live to a ripe old age, she saw many of her efforts for the good of her people carried out to success. She did not spend her long years in vain Though dead, her kind words and thoughtful deeds to the sick and suffering will long be remembered by many of her tenantry. It has been well said —'Good deeds will be as legible on the hearts you leave behind as the stars on the brow of the evening. Good deeds will shine as the stars in Heaven.' So shall it be with the departed Countess of Seafield."

SEAFIELD MEMORIAL CHURCH, GRANTOWN.

An impressive service was held in the Seafield Memorial Church, Grantown. The worshippers, many of whom wore mourning dress, filled the building. Lady Seafield's seat, the pulpit, organ, and communion table were heavily draped in black. The organist, Mr Howat, played as the first voluntary "Andante Religioso," and as the second voluntary Purcell's Dead March Rev. D. Young, minister of the parish, preaching from the words, "Who can find a virtuous woman? for her price is far above rubies," said the death of the Countess of Seafield was a memorable event. So long had she ruled as the lady of the manor, so important the part she had played in the life of that countryside, so familiar her face and figure, so much of a household word her name, that her passing was as when a beech tree fell in the woodland. A gap was left which would not soon be filled. Having recalled a similar service held in Grantown 27 years ago in connection with the funeral obsequies of Ian Charles, 8th Earl of Seafield, Mr Young said the circumstances then were very different to the present. Then it was a young man's funeral, the only son of his mother. A bright and radiant life had closed in circumstances as piteous as well could be imagined, a life full of promise, full of winsomeness, full of high and serious and Christian endeavour. Very different was the life which they commemorated that day. That was the broken Corinthian pillar: this the complete and finished pillar. Lady Seafield's work was done. Her course was finished. The hour for rest had struck. She had come to her grave in a ripe old age, like as a shock of corn in its season. It was an ending, following upon the life it did, such as they could truly say of

Nothing is here for tears, nothing to wail,
Or knock the breast; no weakness, no contempt,
Dispraise or blame—nothing but well and fair,

And what may quiet us in a death so noble. It was a far cry now from the day when the gracious and beautiful girl looked for the first time on the hills of fair Strathspey. She came of an ancient lineage, and who would say that she proved unfaithful to the striking motto of the house of Blantyre—"Sola juvat virtus"—"Virtue alone delights me"? She came to a family whose name for many a generation had been a household word throughout those northern regions. Wide its domains, broad its acres, its estates a little principality, comprising "mountain and forest and sea-kissed plain." It might have been some Laird of

Grant whom Aytoun had in mind when he wrote his well-known lines—

> He kept his castle by the north,
> Hard by the thundering Spey;
> And a thousand vassals dwell around—
> All his lineage they

And who would say that she proved unfaithful to the no less striking motto of the family she came to—"Stand fast, Craigellachie"? She stood fast in her piety, her simple goodness, her womanly sympathy, her affection for the people committed to her care, and her desire to serve their interests. Her life was lengthened beyond the common, and, as was often the case with long lives, it had more than its share of sorrow and sadness It was hard to escape a certain sense of loneliness as one thought of the aged lady up there in the great house of Grant. It was now a generation since she lost her husband, a man greatly beloved, and described as the best of landlords the noblest of chiefs, the kindest and justest of men. When that sword entered her soul the stricken woman could take comfort in the thought of the filial and deeply affectionate son beside her, in whom all her hopes were bound But three years later, when he, too, was taken, and her house was left to her desolate, she must have felt that the light of her life was gone, and that all God's waves and billows had gone over her. "I shall go softly all my years in the bitterness of my soul," she might have cried And she went softly, though not in bitterness. Henceforward she lived a life of comparative seclusion, seeking not the frivolities or pleasures of the gay world, which never had much attraction for her, but content, like the Shunammite of old, to dwell among her own people Among them she lived: among them she died Of her charities and benevolence there was small need for him to speak. Her reputation for benevolence was in all that northern land, although there was much that was never known. She was always thinking of her people, and planning for their good. By personal visits to the homes of the poor, by clubs for providing them with warm and comfortable clothing, by a woman's sympathy, deep and unaffected, with all suffering and all sorrow, by what the poet describes as—

That best portion of a good man's life—
His little, nameless, unremembered acts
Of kindness and of love,

and by princely benefactions she honoured her Master and served her fellow-men.

U.F. CHURCH, GRANTOWN.

In the U.F Church, Grantown, Rev. P T. Hall said in course of his remarks—The angel of death has during the last few days visited cottage and castle. Regarding the lady who has had these lands as a great trust from God for many years we find ourselves wishing that all who hold great positions in our country and great responsibilities might have the same high conscientiousness as the late Lady Seafield had She has had a great task to fulfil under a sense of loss and affliction that shadowed all her days What she had to do was done alone. Doubtless though that made her work harder as a trustee of wide lands, in other ways it fitted her to do that work more worthily and more well, for while it must have laid on her a heavy burden of thought, it must also have opened her heart. Lady Seafield will be mourned deeply among very many of the poor, and one does not know if any of those into whose hands are committed great trusts can leave behind them a sweeter and a nobler memorial than this, that they have remembered the little ones of Christ who have a dwelling by their gates.

BAPTIST CHURCH, GRANTOWN.

Rev. Robert Woodside, Burghead, who officiated in the absence of Rev. D. D. Smith, said that Lady Seafield, though occupying a high social position, was a humble, sincere Christian, of a thoroughly catholic spirit, not confining her munificence to any particular denomination The memory of Lady Seafield would live in the hearts of those for whom she had done so much.

ADVIE PARISH CHURCH.

In Advie Parish Church, Rev. J. Liddell said in course of his remarks—I have a vivid remembrance of the strong impression Lady Seafield's gracious and kindly presence made upon me when I first came among you, and had the honour of being introduced to her who was in a measure your head and chieftainess. She seemed to me to be essentially the great lady, grande dame, as the French say, a lady with great ideals and an earnest purpose to worthily act the high role to which her destiny had called her She was a profoundly religious woman, a true and devoted daughter of the Church of Scotland, like all the race from which she sprang and the race with which she intermarried She was kindness itself to her tenantry and long-suffering to a degree, ever ready to help in bad seasons by remissions of rent, and indulgent to those who had fallen on evil times from their untoward circumstances She never turned any from their homes who were willing to do anything to help themselves, and, a widow herself, she proved herself throughout her long life to be the widow's stay and the orphan's shield. She was, I am told, almost adored by her personal servants and those who came into intimate contact with her The poor and the needy had also in her a ready helper, and the help she gave was ever in the way of helping the poor to help themselves and so allow them to maintain their own self-respect. The fine hospital in Grantown is a fitting memorial of her sincere solicitude for the sick and the suffering And above all, she offered to us all, rich and poor alike, the great example of a good, a pious, a religious life She rests from her labours, but her works do follow her.

CROMDALE PARISH CHURCH.

In Cromdale Parish Church, Rev T. S. Cargill preached from the words, "Lord, now lettest Thou Thy servant depart in peace" He said—The Countess Dowager of Seafield was a great personality. Her strong individuality has impressed itself deep upon the thought and speech of Strathspey, so that all men may know of it. Her gracious life and her intense interest in her responsibilities are not to be measured as things in themselves. They live still, and will live in the unconscious influence they have upon us all. Those who knew Lady Seafield loved her for herself. She had her own share of sorrow, when death took all that was dearest to her, and broke off her purposes in the midst. But not the weight of sorrow nor the burden of years could embitter her soul or rob her of her interest in the duties of life. Now with us is left the memory of a long life well lived, and a great duty well done. She is with God—at rest.

U.F CHURCH, CROMDALE.

In the U.F. Church, Cromdale, Rev. W. B. Gall said the name and influence of Lady Seafield had extended far beyond these ancestral domains She counted it a privilege to dwell among her people and to minister to them. It was her lot to travel through the dark shadow of bereavement, but the spirit of this noble woman rose above her sorrow. Her beautiful Christ-like example made them rejoice in that she had died in the Lord, and that her works did follow her.

PARISH CHURCH, ABERNETHY.

In Abernethy Parish Church, Rev Dr Robertson said—The little I saw of Lady Seafield left upon me the impression that she was a woman of ability, and a good woman who tried to live her life and do her duty as in God's sight. She occupied a position that was admittedly difficult—difficult under any circumstances for a woman, and particularly difficult at the present time, when the old order of things is changing and giving place to new. I believe that the universal opinion is that she was a good landowner, always just to her tenants and often generous. For a long period, owing to increasing years and infirmities, it was impossible for her to have much direct intercourse with the people on her wide estates, but I believe she was always interested in their welfare, and, when cases of suffering or need were brought under her notice, ever ready to help. I have no doubt that there are many to-day who will recall kindnesses received at her hands, and who will feel that by her death they have lost a benefactress and friend.

U.F. CHURCH, ABERNETHY.

In Abernethy U.F. Church, Rev A M'Lean said—Lady Seafield inherited great traditions, and in the eyes of her tenantry she lived up to them In the management of her large estates she could justly be characterised as a model landowner She had a deep sense of her stewardship, and ever sought to live for the good of her people Having herself drunk deeply of the cup of sorrow, she was ever ready to sympathise with those who were in affliction The poor and the needy were the objects of her special care She goes down to the grave in ripe old age, honoured by all who knew her and loved by all who served her. She now rests from her labours, and her works do follow her

KINCARDINE PARISH CHURCH

In Kincardine Parish Church, Rev J. C Maclellan, preaching from the words "A mother in Israel," said Lady Seafield was a woman whose influence was always exerted for the highest and noblest ends, and who sweetened and kept sweet the breath of society Combining in herself high rank and the noblest womanhood, her life was in some respects a sad and pathetic one. Mistress of great wealth and broad acres, it was yet a lonely life Bearing the adverse blows of fate with Christian and Spartan fortitude, her womanhood went out in fullest measure to the humblest, the poor, and the needy. Free from all meanness and narrowness, full of all good works, she lived the simple life in high station; one who did justly, loved mercy, and walked humbly with her God

TRIBUTES BY PUBLIC BODIES.

Tributes to the memory of the Countess of Seafield were made by many public bodies

BANFFSHIRE COUNTY COUNCIL.

A meeting of Banffshire County Council was held at Banff on the 17th, Dr Campbell, Old Cullen, presiding

Sir John Innes said—Before proceeding with the business on the card I think it would be your wish that the Council should put on record the deep feeling of regret everywhere felt at the great loss the county has sustained by the death of the late Lady Seafield. She was the largest landowner in Banffshire, and during the twenty-seven years that she owned the property she managed it with an ability and liberality that gained for her the respect and admiration of all who lived under her The fishermen also in the numerous towns and villages along the extensive coast line of the Seafield property were not forgotten by the late Lady Seafield, and her handsome donations and subscriptions towards the improvement of their harbours added greatly to and increased their prosperity and welfare and increased the wealth of the county. The late Lady Seafield was a person of great individuality. Her interests were wide, and she knew about and formed very clear and decided views on most things. In county business she was much interested, and was quite conversant with all that was being done. In all public affairs where subscriptions were required for a worthy object Lady Seafield was a generous giver, and she will be missed by the residents on her large estates and not least by the poor (Cheers.) I move that "the County Council express their deep regret at the loss the community of Banffshire has sustained in the death of Lady Seafield whose many activities as a great and enlightened landowner advanced the best interests of the county in many ways, and resolve to record in their minutes their sympathy with her relatives, and with the Convener of the county who has been so long associated with her ladyship in her great work, and that an excerpt from this minute be sent to her ladyship's relatives"

Dr M'Killigin seconded.

Mr William Robertson—With your permission I should just like to add a word to what Sir John has so well and so fittingly said with reference to the late Countess Dowager of Seafield She owned very wide and very valuable estates, a very considerable proportion of which lay within Banffshire, and that makes it right and proper and fitting that at this meeting the members of the County Council should join in expressing their appreciation of the worth and character of the late Countess, and of their sympathy with her relatives I could not say that I enjoyed the personal acquaintance of her ladyship, but I know from report that she possessed a clear and intelligent head and a very warm heart. She enjoyed, too, the respect of the community generally, together with the warmest love of those who knew her personally.

The motion was unanimously agreed to.

Dr Campbell—Considering that I have been so closely associated with Lady Seafield during the past twenty-three years in the administration of her affairs, and that I have during all that time had the honour of her friendship and confidence, it is peculiarly gratifying to me that the Council has paid this unanimous tribute of respect to her useful and honourable life.

ELGINSHIRE COUNTY COUNCIL.

A meeting of the Elginshire County Council was held on the 16th, Mr G R Mackessack of Ardgye, convener of the county, presiding.

The Convener, in the course of an eloquent speech, referred to the late Caroline Countess Dowager of Seafield by whose death the county had sustained a great loss. Her ladyship had not only adorned her high position by her personal character, but also by the enlightened and beneficent management of her extensive territorial interests in that county, and by her practical sympathy in the well-being of her tenantry, she had made herself universally beloved and respected by the whole community. He moved that the Council record in their minutes their sense of the great loss the county had sustained, and their sympathy with her relatives in their bereavement, and instruct that an excerpt of the minute be sent to the proper quarter.

This was at once agreed to

ABERDEEN SYNOD

At a meeting of the Synod of Aberdeen on the 10th, Professor Cowan said he was sure all the members would approve of his giving expression to the deep regret they all felt at the death of the distinguished and devoted member of the Church of Scotland, who was one of the patronesses and one of the most generous supporters of the Synod of Aberdeen Auxiliary and of the Sialkot Mission. He need hardly say he referred to the late Countess of Seafield, who endeared herself to the entire community of the north-east of Scotland by her amiable disposition, by her devout character, by her educational zeal and liberality in the spirit of her ancestors, to whom, as they all knew, they owed such valuable educational foundations, and by her warm interest in and support of Christian work, missionary and philanthropic, connected with the Church of Scotland, of which she was so devoted an adherent. Had he been speaking of the endowment scheme he would have testified to the munificence of Lady Seafield in connection both with that scheme and the home mission scheme. They all knew they owed to her munificence the building and part endowment of Inverallan, and the endowment entirely of the parish of Seafield within their own bounds, and every enterprise of the Church of Scotland and religious enterprise of the wider Church of Christ were ever deeply indebted to Lady Seafield's interest, sympathy, and munificent liberality.

Dr Bruce, Banff, said he would like to add his tribute to that of Profesor Cowan to the late Dowager Countess of Seafield. Lady Seafield was always a most kind friend to the

Church, especially with regard to the erection and endowment of parishes and the carrying out of spiritual work there. She was a great friend to education, and took the highest interest in the welfare of all the tenantry on her large estates. She cared for both the spiritual interests and the physical comforts of her people, and at all times maifested her interest in the kindest way, and often in a way that was not seen She was patron of his own parish, and he owed to her his presentation to that living. Dr Bruce also referred to the interest which Lady Seafield took in the work of Sunday Schools.

BANFF TOWN COUNCIL

At a special meeting of Banff Town Council held on the 9th—Provost Christie presiding—a motion of condolence was passed on the death of the Dowager Countess of Seafield and arrangements were made for the attendance of the Council at the funeral ceremonies

The Provost said he had called them together that day because he felt sure that they would all wish to express the deep regret of the Town Council and community of Banff at the great loss the North of Scotland had sustained in the death of the Countess Dowager of Seafield It was now just over twenty-seven years since her son, the 8th Earl of Seafield, suddenly and unexpectedly died. For all these twenty-seven years her ladyship had managed the vast Seafield estates to which she succeeded in a manner which had highly commended itself to all classes and interests Constantly residing on her great estates, she had been a model landowner and the great and permanent improvements she had carried out in the interests of her farmers, the farm-labourers, and her feuars were well known to them all, and would be a monument of her wise and enlightened management. (Hear, hear) Her ladyship had considerable interests in Banff. She had always been a good friend of their Royal Burgh and a kindly neighbour (Hear, hear) He might mention that the Town Council had now for over twenty years had a pleasant association with her ladyship in the administration.

of the Redhythe and Smith educational funds at Fordyce. He might also mention, as an example of the many beneficent acts she had done for their town, her granting for the nominal sum of 1s the site of the Campbell Hospital, an institution in which the Town Council had an important interest. Many such beneficent acts as this had characterised her actions all over her great estates. Her devotion to her high ideal of duty, her great wisdom in the management of her great trusts, her great charity, and her great modesty with it all, would ensure that her memory would be always treasured and held dear by the varied and extensive communities she was so long and so intimately connected with (Hear, hear.) He moved that they as a Council express their deep sense of the loss the community had sustained in the death of her ladyship and their sympathy with her relatives, and that an excerpt from that minute be sent to them. He would also move that they attend the funeral in their corporate capacity. He also moved that the town's bell be tolled on Wednesday and Thursday, and that the town's flag be hoisted half-mast.

Bailie Cumming seconded the resolution. He desired to associate himself with all that had been so fittingly said by the Provost. They deeply regretted the death of Lady Seafield, and they extended to her relatives the Council's sympathy in their bereavement. For over twenty-seven years Lady Seafield had successfully guided the destinies of the wide Seafield estates, but long before she assumed control of these estates she had by her many acts of kindness and beneficence endeared herself to the tenantry, and each year as it passed only tended to deepen and strengthen the bond of sympathy and affection thus established. Living constantly upon her estates she came frequently into personal contact with her tenantry, and to no reasonable request preferred by her tenantry, whether collectively or individually, did she ever turn a deaf ear. Moreover she always endeavoured to make her people's interests her own. For the poor and the sick she had especial care, and no appeal which had for its object the alleviation of the lot of the poor and the suffering was ever made to her in vain Throughout her wide domains she would be very greatly missed, and he was sure that all they in Banff deeply sympathised with her relatives in their bereavement. Her memory would long be held in fragrant and grateful remembrance and her name would be cherished as an enlightened and beneficent landowner who realised to the full the responsibilities and duties of her high position and who discharged these duties unostentatiously, but none the less nobly and well

The Provost's motion was unanimously agreed to, and arrangements were made for attendance at the funeral

CULLEN TOWN COUNCIL

At a meeting of Cullen Town Council on the 13th, Provost Gregor, before commencing the business of the meeting, made reference to the death of the Countess of Seafield, and proposed the following resolution —

"The Provost, Magistrates and Councillors of the Royal Burgh of Cullen resolve to place on record an expression of the deep sorrow which they and the entire community feel on the occasion of the removal by death of the Right Honourable Caroline Countess Dowager of Seafield. The Council are highly sensible of the estimable virtues which adorned her ladyship's character As the proprietrix, for a lengthy period, of vast estates, she was ever conscious of the immense responsibility attaching to her high station Kind and indulgent to her tenants, she took a lively concern in their happiness and welfare

"To Cullen her ladyship was, indeed, a liberal benefactress. Any scheme which had for its object the good and prosperity of the burgh received her warmest sympathy and practical support, and the many privileges enjoyed at her hands were highly prized by the whole community

"So long as she found strength to go amongst her people, she brightened with her sweet presence the homes of the poor, the aged, and the sick. When declining years and weakness came upon her, she was yet mindful of those whose circumstances required her care and support By her many acts of benevolence she earned the gratitude of the inhabitants of Cullen, by whom she will be long and affectionately remembered.

"The Council further record their sincere sympathy and condolence with Her Ladyship's relatives in their sorrowful bereavement"

The resolution was unanimously adopted, and the Clerk was instructed to send an excerpt from the minute to Mr James Campbell, LL D , factor, Old Cullen, for submission to her ladyship's relatives

KEITH TOWN COUNCIL.

A meeting of Keith Town Council was held on the 9th. Provost Cameron presiding

Before commencing the business, the Provost referred to the death of the Countess Dowager of Seafield As the owner of great estates in the county she had held a high position, and one of great influence, not only amongst her own tenantry but also in the general community However great had been her ladyship's responsibilities and opportunities of doing good, still greater had been her ability and desire to do for every good and charitable work all that was required of her. The Countess was idolised by her tenants, especially that class known as small tenants, who had the greatest regard for her and who never trusted in vain to her liberality and kindness of heart. As Superior of Keith they were under many obligations to her. Her help when it was required for any good or useful work was always given with willingness and great liberality They owed to her kindly interest and forethought that princely gift the Seafield Park and plantations, and also the customs of the town. He submitted the following motion— "That there be recorded in the Council's minute the sorrow of the Council and of the whole community at the great loss the town of Keith has sustained through her ladyship's death. Lady Seafield had been Superior of Keith for a long period of years, and always acted with much generosity towards the town in many improvements and in many questions in which the town was interested, particularly in questions of water supply." The motion was seconded by Bailie Stewart and unanimously agreed to, and the Clerk was instructed to send an excerpt to Dr Campbell, her ladyship's factor.

The magistrates and town clerk were appointed a deputation to represent the Council and community at the funeral. It was agreed to toll both the Institution and Parish Church bells during the hour of funeral, and also that the official flags be flown half-mast.

PORTSOY TOWN COUNCIL

A special meeting of Portsoy Town Council was held on the 9th It was moved by Bailie Gray, seconded by Bailie Macdonald, and unanimously agreed to, "That the Town Council of the burgh of Portsoy, having heard with regret of the demise of the Right Honourable Caroline Countess Dowager of Seafield, the superior of the town, resolve to put on record their appreciation and acknowledgment of her ladyship's many acts of benevolence; and to respectfully tender their sympathy and condolence with her ladyship's relatives in their bereavement, and, further, that an excerpt from the Council's minute be forwarded to her relatives at Cullen House"

FORRES TOWN COUNCIL

From the Forres Town Council there was sent the following letter.—

Council Chambers,
Forres, 17th October 1911

My Lord,—I am directed by the Town Council of Forres to convey to you their great regret at the death of the Right Honourable the Dowager Countess of Seafield, and their sympathy with your lordship and the other relatives in your bereavement The Castle Grant family were for many years connected with and interested in the municipal life of this town, and the kindliest feelings have always been entertained by our townspeople towards the family, and to none more so than to the late Countess The Town Council accordingly desire to place on record their sense of the great loss they and so many in the northern counties have sustained by the Countess's death.—I have the honour to be, my Lord, your lordship's obedient servant,

(Sd.) Robert Urquhart.

The Right Honourable The Earl of Cassillis,
Cullen House, Cullen.

ROTHES TOWN COUNCIL.

Excerpt from minute of meeting of the Provost, Magistrates, and Councillors of the burgh of Rothes held on 9th October 1911—

The Provost, magistrates and councillors of the burgh of Rothes for themselves and for the community which they represent resolve to place on record the sense of the great loss sustained by the community of Rothes through the removal by death of the Right Honourable Caroline Countess Dowager of Seafield, and also their sympathy and condolence with her bereaved relatives

Lady Seafield has during the long period of her proprietorship of the Seafield estates evinced a very deep solicitude for the welfare of her tenantry, whose interests she has always regarded as her own, and she has given practical and lasting evidence of her interest in the burgh of Rothes by making generous provision for the enjoyment of healthy recreation by its inhabitants. The handsome donations which her ladyship annually made for the care of the sick and the poor of the community will also be held in long and grateful remembrance.

The Town Council direct the Provost and the Town Clerk to subscribe and transmit a copy of this resolution to David T. Samson, Esq., her ladyship's factor, for submission to her ladyship's relatives.

GRANTOWN TOWN COUNCIL.

A special meeting of Grantown Town Council was held on the 9th, when it was agreed to recommend to the townspeople that all places of business be closed on Thursday from 11 o'clock a.m., and the councillors arranged to attend the funeral in their corporate capacity.

Provost Barclay said—It would be only fitting to make an allusion to our profound sorrow at the death of Lady Seafield. She passed away in a quiet sleep that she had so often wished for Ever since I have known Lady Seafield she has had no desire to live. Her broken heart was for many long years with her husband and her only son in the lonely tomb in Duthil, and in following them there she has gained the desire of her heart. Had she lived a day longer she would have attained to the 60th anniversary of her son's birth What she has been to her tenantry on her vast estates I need not say here. She discharged her various duties from the highest motives, and to many of the poor and afflicted she has been more than a mother. In her life she was an example to the whole community for the high moral tone of her home and for her industry in doing good works. She was always loyal to her late husband and son as heads of the Clan Grant, and her recent efforts to retain the Academy at Fordyce were simply the carrying out of what they had fought for before her. In many homes throughout Strathspey one hears some simple story of her kindness and generosity Perhaps her greatest work of philanthropy and charity was the erection of the "Ian Charles" Hospital, as it will live throughout all time to benefit the sick and afflicted, and as an institution it is being appreciated more and more. Her interest in it was intense She was incessantly making some small gift or garment for the inmates She never grudged any expense in connection with the patients, and if removal to a city hospital was necessary, she paid all outlay. Whatever she thought right, whether it was politic or not, she carried it out, for she feared no one. Whoever follows her in administering those estates with their tremendous responsibilities cannot do better than she did in her acts and intentions towards the tenantry. We will welcome and co-operate with him who succeeds her in doing everything for the furtherance of the good of this community, and for this Grantown and this Strathspey, which have a great future before them. (Applause.)

Bailie Grant said they all agreed with what had been said, and said so well, by the Provost No one was better qualified to speak of her deeds of benevolence than Dr Barclay, and although they had not known in the same intimate way of her good works, they had known much The Council agreed with and endorsed the tribute paid to her ladyship's memory. (Hear, hear.)

BANFF BURGH SCHOOL BOARD.

A meeting of Banff Burgh School Board was held on the 9th, Mr James Grant, solicitor, presiding.

The Chairman said that before beginning the business of the meeting he thought they would wish to express their deep regret at the passing away of the Countess Dowager of Seafield on Friday last full of years and honour. As apart from her wise administration of her rich and very extensive estates, which increased the trade and wealth of the community, and in which their burgh shared, her ladyship took a very keen and active interest in education Now for more than twenty years Banff Burgh School Board had been closely associated with her in the administration of the largest secondary bursary fund in the North of Scotland—the Redhythe and Smith bursaries—held at Fordyce. When their secondary school at Banff was erected on its present site, over which her ladyship held the superiority, the Board obtained every reasonable facility in connection with the same. Many other instances could be given of her great interest in education. The Countess of Seafield was a true lady of innate modesty and singleness of purpose, and very charitable, and administered her vast estates with consummate wisdom. They would never see her like again. He thought it appropriate they should record in their minutes the deep sense of loss the community had sustained in her death.

Rev. A. Boyd seconded, and the Clerk was instructed to send an excerpt to the relatives through Dr Campbell, factor.

BOYNDIE SCHOOL BOARD.

A meeting of Boyndie School Board was held

at Birchwood on the 9th, Mr Geo. Smith, Ordens, presiding over a full attendance of members

The Chairman said before commencing the business of the meeting that day he wished to say a few words about the late Countess of Seafield He was sure it was with sincere sorrow they all heard on Friday of her ladyship's death The last time he had the honour of talking to her was when she selected a site for the Blairmaud school. Her extreme age prevented her from again coming to see its completion, but though unable to come amongst them they knew and felt that her interest in all their educational affairs was as keen as ever The parish mourned the loss of such a generous Christian gentlewoman. (Hear, hear) He moved that they record in their minutes a sense of the loss the parish had sustained by her death, and that an excerpt be sent to Dr Campbell for presentation to the proper quarter (Hear, hear.)

Mr Forbes, Rettie, seconded Lady Seafield, he said, always took a deep interest in their educational affairs Her ladyship had been closely associated with the Redhythe bursaries and they knew that these were of great interest to her. (Hear, hear)

All the members concurred in the resolution and it was unanimously passed.

FORDYCE SCHOOL BOARD

A meeting of Fordyce School Board was held at Portsoy on the 9th, Mr William Forbes, Cowhythe, presiding

The Chairman said—Before beginning the regular business of the meeting, I would like with your permission, to refer to the lamented death of the Dowager Countess of Seafield. In connection with the education of this parish the Countess and her forbears in the Seafield estates have for many long years taken a great and deep interest, particularly in the administration of the Redhythe bursaries held within our parish You all know how her husband successfully retained these bursaries for the students in the north, when the professors of the university wanted to divert them for other purposes, and how when the tenantry and others in the north presented him with a testimonial showing their gratitude for his services in this matter, he gave the money to found two gold medals at the university. (Hear, hear.) The Reidhaven majority bursary was also founded by her son, the eighth Earl. Continuing the traditions of her husband and son, the late Countess, now over twenty years ago, was able in spite of great difficulty, to retain the bursary endowments to the parish of Fordyce. (Hear, hear) I therefore think that it is highly appropriate that our Board should express a deep sense of their regret at her lamented death, and convey their sympathy to her relatives I beg to move accordingly, and that an excerpt of this minute be sent to the relatives.

Bailie Gray said he had great pleasure in seconding the motion. This was not the time to recall the fact that there was a difference between Lady Seafield and them, but he believed her interest in education was as honest and consistent as their own. They had differed certainly on the question as to where the school should be, but he believed that Lady Seafield's opinion was held as strongly and honestly as they held the opposite. He had therefore pleasure in seconding the motion.

The motion was agreed to.

CULLEN SCHOOL BOARD.

A meeting of the School Board of Cullen was held on the 16th. Rev W G. G M'Lean in the chair.

The Chairman, before commencing the ordinary business of the meeting, suitably referred to the death of the Countess Dowager of Seafield, and proposed the following resolution—" The School Board of Cullen resolve to record in their minutes their deep sense of loss at the death of the Countess Dowager of Seafield, who had always taken a keen interest in education and had never failed, when opportunity offered, to use her influence and give of her means to strengthen the hands of School Boards and teachers in their efforts to reach and maintain a high standard of efficiency in the schools of the parishes throughout her estates. The School Board further record their sincere sympathy with her ladyship's relatives in their sad bereavement."

The resolution was unanimously agreed to, and the Clerk was instructed to send an excerpt from this minute to James Campbell, Esq , LL D , factor, Old Cullen, for submission to her ladyship's relatives.

DESKFORD PARISH COUNCIL

A meeting of the Parish Council of Deskford was held in the school of Deskford on the 10th. In the unavoidable absence of Dr Campbell, Rev George M Park was called to the chair.

The Chairman said before commencing the business of the meeting he thought the Parish Council of Deskford should resolve to record their deep sense of the great loss which the parish and district had sustained in the death of Caroline Dowager Countess of Seafield, in whom the poor had always a warm and generous benefactress, and whose policy it was to promote the happiness and welfare of her people. They recognise that in her they had a most liberal proprietrix, who took a keen and enlightened interest in all that pertained to the moral and social wellbeing of her tenantry, and whose generosity has done so much within recent years to increase the prosperity of the inhabitants of the parish.

The resolution was agreed to, and the Clerk was instructed to forward an excerpt of the minute to Dr Campbell for presentation to the relatives

CROMDALE PARISH COUNCIL.

A meeting of Cromdale Parish Council was held at Grantown on the 11th, Mr George Barclay, chairman of the Council, presiding

The Chairman said—Before taking up the business of this meeting you will expect and desire that I should refer to the event which has been so much in our minds since we heard of the death of the Countess Dowager of Seafield on Friday. Before the majority of us were born Lady Seafield was an influence in Strathspey, and her passing has broken a link that united us in many happy memories and tender associations with the simple and sincere lives of our fathers. It was the traditional policy of the house of Grant to have a prosperous and contented people within their wide domain, and when, on the death of her son, the burden of administering the Seafield estates fell on her shoulders, she braced herself to discharge in the same spirit the great trust with a courage, fidelity, and wise discrimination that have been extolled in the press and from the pulpit. Like her predecessors, she lived amongst her own people, ever realising the spirit of the old motto, "Noblesse oblige," that nobility imposes obligations. Those who knew her extolled her wise converse, her modesty, and the sweet mellowness and kindliness of her disposition, but what most strongly appeals to us as a body entrusted with the relief of the poor was her overflowing and active sympathy with the poor and the suffering, and her large beneficence in ministering to their necessities. The Ian Charles Hospital, erected and endowed by her, is an enduring memorial of her bounty and charity Lady Seafield has gone from us with the falling of the leaf and in the fulness of a ripe and honoured old age I move that we record in our minutes our profound sense of the loss the parish and community have sustained in the death of Lady Seafield, and that we send an excerpt of this minute, with an expression of sympathy and condolence, to her relatives.

This was agreed to.

ABERDEEN-ANGUS CATTLE SOCIETY.

A meeting of the Council of the Aberdeen-Angus Cattle Society was held in Aberdeen on October 26. Sir John Macpherson Grant, Bart, of Ballindalloch, president of the Society, presided, and there were also present Mr T. F. Inkson, Kinermony; Mr F G M'Conachie, Ardoch; Mr John Michie, Balmoral; Mr Claude Ralston, Glamis House; Mr Jas. Whyte, Hayston; and Mr Wm. Wilson, Coynachie and Tochineal. Before the business of the meeting was commenced, the Chairman made reference to the death of the Countess of Seafield, and moved the following resolution:—

"The Council of the Aberdeen-Angus Cattle

Society desire to place on record their sense of the great loss sustained by the death of the Countess Dowager of Seafield Her ladyship had been a member of the Society since 1884, when she succeeded her son, the late Earl of Seafield, who was also a member of the Society, and who founded the herd of Aberdeen-Angus cattle in 1882 The Council further desire to place on record their appreciation of the valuable services rendered to Aberdeen-Angus cattle by the late Countess of Seafield through the maintenance of a large and fine herd of the breed, representatives of which won highest honours both at the leading summer and winter shows of the United Kingdom, the Smithfield champion of 1908 having been bred at and exhibited from Cullen House They further desire to express their sympathy with the relatives of the deceased Lady Seafield, and direct that an excerpt from this minute be forwarded by the secretary to them"

Mr William Wilson seconded, and the motion was unanimously agreed to.

CENTRAL BANFFSHIRE FARMER CLUB

The committee of the Club met at Keith on the 21st. Mr James Davidson, Newton of Cairnie, presiding

Before commencing the business, the Chairman said he thought they would agree that they should, as a committee of the Club, record the sense of the deep loss they had sustained in the death of the great and good lady, the Countess of Seafield. Those of them who were tenants on that estate knew that they had lost a most generous and sympathetic landowner, and they as a Club were the poorer to-day inasmuch as they had lost one who, both as a breeder and exhibitor of rare merit and as a most generous patroness of their Club and donor to their prize funds, made the welfare of her tenants and the cause of agriculture generally one of the greatest aims of her long life.

Messrs George Cameron and John M'Pherson also gave expression to the loss felt by the death of Lady Seafield. and on the motion of the Chairman it was agreed to send an excerpt from the minutes to Dr Campbell.

FORRES AND NORTHERN FAT CATTLE CLUB.

The following minute was adopted by the committee of this club:—

The committee of the Forres and Northern Fat Cattle Club desire to place on record the expression of their deep regret at the loss which the county has sustained by the death of the Countess Dowager of Seafield. One of the largest landowners in the county, Lady Seafield was universally recognised as a benevolent and considerate proprietrix, and was deservedly revered and esteemed by her numerous tenantry and feuars Amongst the many objects which shared her ladyship's kind and bountiful consideration, Lady Seafield was for many years a patroness of this Club, and a generous contributor to its prizelist, and was also a welcome and successful exhibitor at its annual shows The committee desire most respectfully to express their sympathy with the late Lady Seafield's relatives, and instruct that an excerpt of this minute be sent to Dr Campbell

Signed in name and on behalf of the committee by

John Mavor, Convener
Alex Dunbar, Secretary

CULLEN CURLING CLUB.

The annual meeting of the Cullen Curling Club was held on the 20th, Mr James Mackenzie presiding. Before commencing the business of the meeting, the Chairman, in feeling terms, alluded to the sad loss the club had sustained through the lamented death of the Countess Dowager of Seafield, and moved the following resolution, which was seconded by Mr James Moir, secretary, and unanimously agreed to—"That this meeting place on record an expression of deep regret at the passing away of the Right Hon. the Countess Dowager of Seafield, who had filled the office of patroness of the club since its resuscitation in 1895, and who took the greatest interest in all the club's competitions and ofttimes graced the proceedings with her presence. To her ladyship's generosity the club was indebted for the free use at all times of the Cullen House curling pond. There is expressed the club's deepest sympathy with her ladyship's relatives, and it is asked that an excerpt from the minutes be sent to Lord Cassillis, the present patron of the club, on behalf of the relatives"

SEAFIELD MEMORIAL CHURCH, INVERALLAN

Excerpt from minute of meeting of the Trustees of the Seafield Memorial Church, Inverallan, held on 16th October.—

The Trustees desire to take the earliest opportunity of expressing their profound sense of the loss which they and the congregation worshipping in Inverallan Memorial Church have sustained by the lamented death of the Right Honourable the Countess Dowager of Seafield Loved and trusted by her people whose welfare she ever studied, her memory will always be cherished as a friend of the poor. Warmly attached to the Church of Scotland her munificent and much appreciated gift to the parishioners of the Seafield Memorial Church will be a lasting monument to her piety and beneficence. In this church she frequently enjoyed the privilege of Holy Communion with her people to whom she was bound by many enduring ties. The Trustees deeply sympathise and condole with her ladyship's relatives in their loss, and it was agreed to send an extract of this minute to Captain David Baird

(Signed) John Grant, Clerk to the Trustees.

"To Captain David Baird.

"The Kirk Session of Inverallan beg to convey to you, as representing the relatives of the late Right Honourable Countess Dowager of Seafield, an expression of their deep sympathy in your recent bereavement. They would add their share of testimony to the lofty Christian character of Lady Seafield, to her high sense of responsibility, to her manifold benevolence, to her thoughtfulness for the poor and needy, and her sympathy with all in tribulation. They remember the meek and submissive spirit in which she bowed herself to the holy will of God, when, in His inscrutable wisdom, He sent her great and desolating sorrows. Nor can they forget her many services to the Church of Christ, her warm and unaffected interest in all that concerned the good of this parish, in all that pertained to the Kingdom of God. Lady Seafield was ever regular in her attendance on holy ordinances, in this as in other matters setting a noble example in her high and influential station And, finally, the Session would renew their acknowledgment of her generosity and munificence in gifting to the Church of Scotland, in loving memory of her husband and son, the present parish church of Inverallan, in which they have the honour to be office-bearers They rejoice in that Lady Seafield has bequeathed so pure a remembrance, and they render thanks to God for the gift of her whom He has taken unto Himself, and whose loss is universally lamented

"Signed in the name and by the authority of the Kirk-Session of Inverallan.

'David Young, B.D , Moderator.

"Grantown-on-Spey, 25th Oct 1911."

BIRNIE PARISH COUNCIL.

Excerpt from minutes of meeting of the Parish Council of Birnie, held on 27th Oct .—

The Rev. Mr Kennedy moved and it was unanimously resolved.—

That the Council record in their minutes an expression of the deep loss the parish of Birnie has sustained by the death of the Right Hon Caroline Countess Dowager of Seafield, whose removal from their midst carries with it the sense of personal loss, and has awakened throughout the parish feelings of the deepest sorrow and regret.

The considerate and generous policy adopted by Lady Seafield in the management of her extensive estates, her ladyship's solicitude for the welfare and comfort of her tenantry, and the numerous and important improvements she has effected on behalf of the farmers and feuars, have borne fruit in the prosperous condition of the properties to-day, the contentment of the tenantry, and the deep gratitude with which her memory is cherished.

It was fortunate for Birnie, when its ancient and historic church required restoration, that its fate lay so largely in the hands of one so liberal and so warmly attached to the Church of Scotland, and her ladyship's generosity in this matter, as principal heritor in the parish, will never be forgotten

Her high aims, her unselfish life, replete with touching acts of kindness to those in sorrow or in need, marked out her ladyship as not only a model proprietrix, but also as a dignified Christian gentlewoman and a pattern of true nobility.

The Council instruct their Clerk to send an excerpt from the minutes of this meeting to the relatives of Lady Seafield, conveying their respectful sympathy, and expressing the hope that consolation may be afforded them by the unfading memory of the beautiful and beneficent life of her who so worthily upheld the noble traditions of the ancient house and family of Grant

(Signed) Alister J. Morrison, Clerk.
28th October 1911

KEITH CURLING CLUB.

Excerpt from annual general meeting of Keith Curling Club held on 14th October —

"It was unanimously resolved to place on record the sincere sorrow of the members of the Club on the sad occasion of the death of the Right Honourable Caroline Countess Dowager of Seafield The Keith curlers are sensible of the practical interest Lady Seafield took in the welfare of the Club by her generosity in granting a site for the pond and contributing handsomely to the building of the club-house. The curlers respectfully desire to express their sympathy with the relatives of her ladyship, and request Dr Campbell to forward this their humble tribute of respect to them

"Thomas Stewart, Hon. Secy."

GRANTOWN-ON-SPEY AMENITIES COMMITTEE.

Excerpt from minute of meeting of the Grantown-on-Spey Amenities Committee held on 23rd October:—

The vice-convener, Bailie A. F Grant, who

presided, moved—That this Committee express their deep sense of the loss the community of Grantown has sustained in the death of the Countess of Seafield and their sympathy with the relatives.

In submitting the motion, Bailie Grant said —Before beginning the business of the meeting, I feel sure, gentlemen, it is your desire that as a committee we should pay our tribute of respect to the memory of the late Countess of Seafield. We can heartily endorse all that has already been said—and well said—by our Provost and the Chairman of the Parish Council on behalf of our two principal representative bodies Grantown and its amenities are much indebted to successive Lairds of Grant for our beautifully situated town, our fine wide streets, our picturesque square, and the lovely approach from the river to the town, commonly known as the New Road To her late ladyship we are specially indebted for our innumerable walks and paths through these beautiful woods, for the many liberties we enjoy, and for the necessary ground, at a nominal rent, given to our various recreation clubs—our Golf Club, Skating Club, Bowling and Tennis Clubs, &c , all of which are an inestimable boon to our community and greatly valued by our visitors. The late Countess of Seafield was truly a conscientious and generous proprietrix, and withal a faithful steward in her administration of the extensive estates bequeathed to her by her only son, and now that we know that she has handed back these estates by deed of settlement to the House of Grant, nothing could possibly give greater satisfaction to her tenantry and clansmen than this last act of her late ladyship.

The motion, seconded by Mr John S. Grant, was unanimously adopted, and the Secretary was instructed to send an excerpt to the relatives through Mr Smith Grant, factor.

ROTHES BOWLING CLUB.

Excerpt from minute of meeting of the committee of the Rothes Bowling Club held on 25th October:—

"The committee of the Rothes Bowling Club

desire to place on record their sense of the great loss sustained by the Club through the death of the Right Honourable Caroline Countess Dowager of Seafield, and to express their sympathy and condolence with her bereaved relatives When the Club was formed about three years ago, the late Lady Seafield gave practical evidence of her interest in the promotion of healthy recreation for the community by generously fixing a site for the green, by giving a handsome donation to defray the cost of making, and also by her acceptable gift of timber for the erection of the beautiful pavilion which now adorns the Rothes bowling green. Not only did Lady Seafield by her kindly actions make herself the Club's greatest benefactor, but to other institutions in this district was she ever ready and willing to extend a strong and helping hand, and especially where these pertained to the general advancement and welfare of her people. Her kindness of heart and the record of her long and trying life remain in grateful remembrance."

BANFFSHIRE CONSERVATIVE ASSOCIATION.

The annual meeting of the Banffshire Conservative Association was held at Keith on 4th November, His Grace the Duke of Richmond and Gordon, K G , in the chair.

The Duke, before entering on a review of public questions, said he should like to express, as he was sure he did on their behalf, how deeply they felt the loss by death of the Countess of Seafield. Although not, through force of circumstances, an actual member of the Association, still in material ways she was of great assistance to them. (Cheers) He knew he was addressing some of her tenants, and they knew the interest and the solicitude she took in all affairs, public and private, and they as politicians knew the interest which she took in assisting them in endeavouring to provide the county with someone who would represent what she thought were the proper views which should be held on the political questions of the day, so whether they looked at her in a private capacity or at the part, small though it was, that she took in public affairs. he felt they would agree with him when he said that the county of Banff was poorer a great deal by the loss they had sustained. (Cheers.)

NORTHERN SEEDS AND ROOTS ASSOCIATION.

The annual meeting of the Northern Seeds and Roots Association was held at Portsoy on 4th November. Mr George Smith, Ordens, presiding.

Before proceeding to the ordinary business, the Chairman made feeling reference to the loss the Association had sustained through the death of Lady Seafield, and moved.—

"That this annual meeting of the members of the Northern Seeds and Roots Association express their profound sorrow and regret at the lamented death of the Right Honourable Caroline Countess Dowager of Seafield, who since the inception of the Association in 1895 had been Lady Patroness of the Association, and who during all the years of the Association's existence had taken a keen personal interest in all that pertained to its welfare, and had been a very liberal contributor to its funds, that the members of the Association extend their sympathy to the relatives of her ladyship in their sad bereavement; and instruct the Secretary to forward an excerpt from this minute to the relatives through Dr Campbell, Old Cullen."

Ex-Provost Burgess seconded and the motion was unanimously agreed to and adopted.

ROTHES SCHOOL BOARD.

Excerpt from minute of meeting of Rothes School Board held on 3rd November:—

The Chairman submitted the following resolution, viz.—"That the School Board of the parish of Rothes, having learned with the deepest regret that the Right Honourable Caroline Countess Dowager of Seafield passed to her rest upon 6th October, resolve to place upon record in its minutes its sense of the great loss to the community thereby sustained. The School Board is fully aware of the great interest which the Countess Dowager of Seafield has always manifested in everything pertaining to the interests of the parish, and in no matter can it be said that she took a greater interest than in the matter of education The School Board further express its sympathy with the relatives of her family in their present bereavement"

The resolution was unanimously adopted, and the Clerk was instructed to send an excerpt from the minute to Mr Samson to forward to the proper quarter

CULLEN PARISH COUNCIL

Excerpt from minute of meeting of the Parish Council of Cullen held on 8th Nov..—

On the motion of Provost Gregor, seconded by ex-Bailie Brown, it was unanimously resolved that the Council record in their minutes an expression of the deep sorrow felt by the Council on the death of the Right Honourable Caroline Countess Dowager of Seafield, and the irreparable loss the community have sustained through her demise. While Lady Seafield devoted her life to the welfare and comfort of every one on her large estates, her special solicitude was always for the poor and the suffering, to whom she ever extended the most generous help and sympathy. Nowhere has her ladyship's kind bounty been more generously dispensed than in the parish of Cullen, and the great benefits and comfort bestowed on the poor through the Clothing Club so long maintained by Lady Seafield, her seasonable gifts of provisions and coals at the New Year, and her generous support of and great personal interest in the District Nursing Association will ever be held in grateful remembrance by the whole community.

The Council instruct their Clerk to send an excerpt from the minutes of the meeting to Dr Campbell, Old Cullen, to be submitted to Lady Seafield's relatives to whom the Council offer their respectful sympathy in their sad bereavement.

The Council also extended to Dr Campbell their sincere sympathy in the great personal loss which he has sustained through the death of Lady Seafield.

ROTHES CURLING CLUB.

At the annual general meeting of the Rothes Curling Club held in the Town Hall on 24th October, it was unanimously agreed to record in the minutes an expression of the great regret at the loss they had sustained in the death of the Right Hon Caroline Countess Dowager of Seafield. In common with the whole community, the Rothes Curling Club feel the loss of one who took a great interest in them and who, when asked in any way to assist them, responded most generously The President and Secretary were authorised to sign and forward this excerpt to the relatives of the deceased Countess, through David T. Samson, Esq , factor, Elgin.

KEITH PARISH COUNCIL

Excerpt from minutes of meeting of Parish Council of Keith of date 14th November—

On the motion of Mr Cameron, seconded by Mr Ledingham, the Council unanimously agreed to record in their minutes an expression of their deep sense of the loss which the community had sustained through the death of Lady Seafield. Lady Seafield throughout her long life was a generous benefactor to the poor and needy, and through the organisation known as the Clothing Club, Lady Seafield did much in this parish to assist many to provide themselves with clothing, which otherwise could not have been provided. Her many gifts to the the people of Keith will long be remembered.

The Clerk was instructed to send an excerpt minute to Dr Campbell, as representative of the relatives.

BOYNDIE PARISH COUNCIL.

A meeting of the Parish Council of Boyndie was held on November 15—Mr Alex. Murray presiding. Before proceeding with the ordinary business of the meeting, the Chairman, in referring to the loss sustained by the parish in the death of Lady Seafield, made the following motion —That the Council record in their minutes an expression of the regret and sorrow felt by them at the death of the Right Honourable Caroline Countess Dowager of Seafield, and the loss sustained by the community generally, and the tenantry in particular, through her death. The Chairman added that Lady Seafield's devotion to everything that concerned the best interests of all under her, throughout the large estates over which she held sway, was undertaken as a life work. In this district, her Ladyship had left many tokens of her bounty, generously bestowed; and Lady Seafield's valued assistance and interest in the provision of a new harbour for Whitehills would ever be held in grateful remembrance as well as her personal visits amongst many of her tenants The Chairman further moved that an excerpt from the minutes be forwarded to Lady Seafield's relatives, through Dr Campbell, Old Cullen. Mr George Smith seconded, and the motion was unanimously agreed to.

ABERNETHY PARISH COUNCIL.

Excerpt from minute of meeting of Parish Council of Abernethy, held on 14th November— The members of the Parish Council resolve to place on record their deep sense of the great loss the parish has sustained by the death of the Right Honourable Caroline Countess Dowager of Seafield

Since the time her Ladyship came to Strathspey, about sixty years ago, she has been closely identified with all good works affecting the welfare of her people, and her ready sympathy and assistance to the poor and to all in sickness and distress had made her name a household word in many homes.

The members further resolve to transmit a copy of this minute to her Ladyship's relatives, with their respectful sympathy in their bereavement, and instruct the clerk accordingly.

BIRNIE SCHOOL BOARD.

Excerpt from minute of meeting of the School

Board of Birnie held at Elgin on 17th November—

This being the first occasion on which the Board met since the lamented death of the Right Honourable Caroline Countess Dowager of Seafield, it was unanimously resolved on the motion of Mr Hair, seconded by Mr Allan, to record in the minutes an expression of the profound loss the parish of Birnie has sustained by the death of her Ladyship, whose deep interest in all matters pertaining to the social and educational welfare of the inhabitants was constantly maintained since she succeeded to the estates of Seafield and Grant twenty-seven years ago, that the Board desire to convey to the relatives their respectful sympathy and condolence, and instruct the clerk to forward to them an excerpt from this minute.

SCHOOL BOARD OF URQUHART AND GLENMORISTON.

Excerpt from minute of meeting of School Board of Urquhart and Glenmoriston held at Drumnadrochit on November 15—

The Board record their sense of the loss the parish has sustained through the death of Caroline Countess Dowager of Seafield.

They recall with gratitude the interest she and her family took in the education of the young previous to 1872, the subsequent gift of the old school for a library and reading room, the use of a park for sports and recreation, and her unfailing support of the school prize fund.

The Board instruct their clerk to forward an excerpt of this minute to Mr D. T. Samson.

PARISH COUNCIL OF URQUHART AND GLENMORISTON.

Excerpt of the minute of the Parish Council of Urquhart and Glenmoriston, dated 15th November, at the Council Office, Drumnadrochit:—

Before proceeding to the business of the day the Chairman, Mr Grant of Glenmoriston, moved the following resolution, viz.:—

"That this Council record upon their minutes their deep sense of the loss sustained by the Seafield estates, and, in particular, by the Urquhart estate, in the death, on the 6th ult., of Caroline, the Countess Dowager of Seafield. While well aware of the wise and benevolent interest she took in all that concerned the estate and its people, the Council feel that as guardians of the poor it falls to them in a special way to take an appreciative notice of her ladyship's great kindness and generosity to the poor and needy upon the estate. The older members of the Council bear testimony that on coming to the estate, about sixty years ago, she set herself the task of looking after the betterment of the condition of the poor and helpless, and it is now well known that her active benevolence has ever since been continuous and systematic. The Council cannot but think with much regret of the ending of a life so useful, noble, and beautiful, and adorned with so many Christian graces.

The resolution was unanimously adopted, and an excerpt thereof, signed by the Chairman and Clerk, was ordered to be sent to the factor upon the estate, Mr D. T. Samson, for transmission to her Ladyship's relatives.

ROTHES PARISH COUNCIL

Excerpt from minute of meeting of the Parish Council of Rothes held on 9th November.—

The Council resolved to record their sincere regret at the great loss the community has sustained through the removal by death of the Right Honourable Caroline Countess Dowager of Seafield, and also to express their sympathy and condolence with her relatives. During the long period of her proprietorship, Lady Seafield devoted herself to the welfare and comfort of her tenantry and evinced a very deep solicitude for the poor and suffering, by whom her generous help and sympathy will long be remembered.

The Clerk was instructed to transmit an excerpt of this minute to David T. Samson, Esq., Elgin, for submission to her ladyship's relatives.

PRESBYTERY OF FORDYCE.

At a meeting of the Presbytery of Fordyce held at Cullen on 29th November there was adopted a minute in the following terms:—

The Presbytery of Fordyce desire to place on record their sense of the great loss sustained by the death of the Right Honourable Caroline Dowager Countess of Seafield The Church of Scotland had in her a generous and worthy member whose lofty example and sincere piety shed a lustre upon her character and house, and was a stimulus to all with whom she came in contact. The Presbytery cannot forget her generous liberality to many parishes within the bounds and her deep interest in the physical, moral and spiritual wellbeing of all upon her estates and her sympathetic interest in the deserving poor; and they instruct the Clerk to send an extract of this minute to Dr Campbell for transmission to the relatives

PARISH COUNCIL OF DUTHIL AND ROTHIEMURCHUS.

Excerpt from minutes of meeting of the Parish Council of Duthil and Rothiemurchus held at Boat of Garten on 28th October Present—Mr J. P Grant of Rothiemurchus, Chairman, Mr James M'Ainsh, Kinchurdy; Mr Alex. Grant, Dalbuiack; Mr J. Grant Smith, Inverallan; Mr J. M. Allan, Easter Duthil; Mr Wm MacGillivray, Auchterblair; and Mr Jas. Davidson, Aviemore.

The Chairman stated that before proceeding with the formal business of the Council he would move a resolution as follows, viz.:—

"That this Council resolve to record their profound sense of the great loss that this parish and the community have sustained by the death of Caroline Countess of Seafield, to whose kind heart and wise judgment they have been indebted for many benefits during the past sixty-one years, and direct that an extract of this minute be sent to Captain David Baird for conveyance to the family.".

The resolution was unanimously agreed to.

PULPIT REFERENCE.

FORDYCE PARISH CHURCH.

"Leaving us an example that we should follow."—1st Peter ii., 21.

There is, however, one consideration that takes this example left us by Christ out of the region of the unattainable. We have the record of this ideal life lived by Christ himself. We have the record of thousands who in past days lived the Christlike life, but our frailty demands more. Just as it was necessary that the Word should become flesh and tabernacle amongst us if we were to be convinced of the love of God towards us, so here we require the Christlike life lived in our midst to persuade us that the example Christ left us is capable of being realized by human imperfection. And we have seen it exemplified not once but often in the cottage and in the mansion both.

The last week has deprived us of one who was a signal instance. Caroline Countess of Seafield was remarkable for mental attainments and business aptitude far above the average, but she was chiefly remarkable for the fidelity with which she followed in the steps of Christ. We are not here to flatter the great, living or departed, but assuredly we are not here to detract from greatness of those in whom was the true nobility. In her case it was unmistakably present. Following her Lord as she did truly she has left us an example that we should follow. She knew much of sorrow, but it drove her to her Father, not from Him, and made her infinitely pitiful. I need not recall to you her great and practical interest in the poor. I need not remind you that she conducted her great estates as a solemn trust from God. We had no talk under her of rights and privileges. It was all of duties. Landlord and tenant worked harmoniously together for the general good, and there was always respect and affection on both sides so that it was hard to say whether she loved most or was most greatly loved. Her influence was always cast in the scale for purity and uprightness. In devotion to the House of God she was a striking example. Hers was a life beautifully balanced and proportioned, "not slothful in business, fervent in spirit serving the Lord." We shall not look upon her like again, but to-day gratefully and humbly we return thanks to Almighty God for the example she left us—"an example that we should follow."

"Now the labourer's task is o'er," but her example will speak when you and I have entered upon that fuller life which she now inherits.